AMHERST ROTARY GOES TO WAR:
AMHERST ROTARY IN WORLD WAR II

EDITED BY
MASON LOWANCE, JR.

An Off the Common Book, Amherst, Massachusetts

Printed in the United States of America

ISBN: 978-1-62534-402-1

CONTENTS

Editor's Note vii

Introduction 1

Testimony of The Rev. John Balcom 7

Thomas Carhart, USAAF 8

Frank Chapman Testimony 13

John T. Conlon 34

Mike de Sherbinin and World War II 43

Judson C. Ferguson 44

Duncan Fraser 49

War in the Pacific 117

Gerald Grady's Story 119

Robert F. Grose 122

Robert W Lenz 142

Jack Mathews' Story 145

Chester Penza 147

Donald R. Progulske 152

Arthur R. Quinton 159

Tom Quarles Service in World War II 166

Bob Shumway's Story 170

Testimony of Veteran A.P. "Al" Stevens 175

Allen L. Torrey 177

Conrad A. Wogrin 202

"Soldiers: We are to be congratulated because we have been chosen as the units of the United States Army best trained to take part in this great American effort...When the great day of battle comes, remember your training and above all that speed and vigor of attack are the sure roads to success, and you must succeed —for to retreat is as cowardly as it is fatal. Indeed, once landed, retreat is impossible. Americans do not surrender.

During the first few days and nights after you get ashore, you must work unceasingly, regardless of sleep, regardless of food. A pint of sweat will save a gallon of blood.

The eyes of the world are watching us; the heart of America beats for us; God is with us. On our victory depends the freedom or slavery of the human race. We shall surely win."[1]

"Why, by God, I actually pity those poor sons-of-bitches we're going up against. By God, I do!"

George S. Patton, Jr.

---

1 George S. Patton, Jr. Letter to the invasion force of Operation Torch, The Invasion of North Africa, November 8, 1942. From Martin Blumenson, ed., *1940 The Patton Papers -1945*, p. 37.

EDITOR'S NOTE

"Blood and Guts" Patton was a career Army officer in The Great War, 1914-18, and in World War II. His courage and bravado were legendary and occasionally his outspoken pronouncements outraged his commanding officers. However, he was respected and beloved by the soldiers he led into battle whether in North Africa against Erwin Rommel or in Belgium at Bastogne in the Battle of the Bulge. Like Dwight Eisenhower, Patton believed that the Allied forces were engaged in a "Crusade in Europe" against the forces of evil that were manifested in Hitler and the Nazis. Contemporary war historians like Stephen Ambrose have focused, like Patton, on the lives of ordinary soldiers rather than the strategies of the generals and admirals. As Ambrose put it, "My job is to pick out the best and most representative, the ones that illuminate common themes or illustrate typical actions. Long ago my mentors taught me to let my characters speak for themselves by quoting them liberally. They were there. I wasn't. They saw with their own eyes, they put their own lives on the line. I didn't. They speak with an authenticity no one else can match. Their phrases, their word choices, their slang are unique - naturally enough, as their experiences were unique. As much as the Civil War soldiers, the GIs believed in their cause. They knew they were fighting for decency and democracy and they were proud of it and motivated by it. They just didn't talk or write about it. (Now) they speak with their own voices and in their own words."[2]

---

2   Stephen Ambrose, *Citizen Soldiers, the U.S. Army from the Normandy Beaches to the Bulge to the Surrender or Germany, June 7, 1944 to May 7, 1945.* (New York: Simon and Shuster, 1997). From the Prologue.

The editor has attempted to follow the guidelines and examples of Stephen Ambrose in the gathering of World War II narratives from the living members of the Amherst Rotary Club. Each contribution originated in an oral presentation at club meetings in 1995 that were dedicated to the anniversary of the end of World War II in 1945. Most contributors had not spoken much about their wartime experiences and most had returned from the war to get on with their civilian lives. Therefore, the new generation of Amherst Rotarians, like myself, had to engage these veterans in lunch table conversations about the war to learn what our colleagues had experienced from 1941-1945. In the late 1990s at least one table of veterans would dine together and share some of their war stories. A Xeroxed version of this book appeared in 2003, after the editor had been able to solicit a number of contributions from both theaters of the war, the European as well as the Pacific. All of those copies were sold almost immediately, and in 2018, the Amherst Rotary Board voted to produce a proper book containing the personal testimonials of our members who had served in World War I1. Several Amherst Rotary Presidents have been extremely supportive of this project, including Arthur Quinton, Justine Holdsworth, Leslie Smith, and Robert Berman. Duncan Fraser, who appears on the book's cover, solicited testimonies and typed several entries on his computer. Connie Wogrin, USA, not only landed at Normandy in 1944 to establish a communications center on the beachhead there; he also returned to Chair the Department of Computer Science at Yale and to found the department at the University of Massachusetts. To the veterans themselves goes the most praise; without their willingness to share these testimonials it would have been impossible to develop this book. As editor, I am grateful to each veteran for his hard work and military service, narrative text and photographs.

Semper Fidelis Mason I. Lowance, Jr. 2018

AMHERST ROTARY GOES TO WAR: AMHERST ROTARY IN WORLD WAR II

The document that follows has been inspired by several recent developments that highlight America's participation in World War II. First, in 1995, the Amherst Rotary Club memorialized the fiftieth anniversary of the ending of World War II by devoting four months of its programs to presentations by members who had served in that war. There were at that time some twenty-five active Rotarians in Amherst who were in the armed services during World War II, and most of these made presentations to the club about their experiences. Three Army members had landed at Normandy in the days following June 6, 1944, and several more had proceeded across Europe to the Battle of the Bulge. Several were aviators, one flying P-38s as bomber escort in raids over Germany; another flying C-47s in England, France, and Germany, and a third transporting President Franklin Roosevelt to and from the Casablanca conference aboard a Navy-Pan American Clipper, twice crossing the Atlantic. Many members were in the Navy during the conflict, serving mainly in the Pacific theater, and one of our Rotary Club presidents served in the Royal Navy in the Atlantic. A naval officer and a Marine discovered that they had both served in the Okinawa invasion in 1944. According to the son of one Army veteran who is now also a member of Amherst Rotary, these 1995 presentations marked the first time his father had ever spoken about his experience in World War II. Indeed, this theme continued to surface, i.e., the recent opportunity to reflect on the experience of combat during the Second

World War inspired many of the Rotary participants to develop narratives of their past service.

The second development behind this book is the sad awareness that we are rapidly losing veterans of World War II at an alarming rate. According to the former Secretary of Veterans Affairs, Anthony J. Principi, there were some eighteen million men and women in the armed services between 1941 and 1945, of whom only five million are still living. Principi also stated that this group is being diminished at the rate of some one thousand to twelve hundred persons per day.

Obviously, the gathering of information and interviewing of our Rotary veterans was an important consideration in the timing of this publication. In the same spirit, the Office of Veterans Affairs in Washington has established several hundred centers around the United States, to which veterans may go to be interviewed for an Oral History Project that tape records and preserves testimonials and memories of the events of 1941-1945. (The Veterans History Project is a national program led by the American Folklife Center at the Library of Congress). This book will become part of that record at the Library of Congress.

Finally, the publication of newsman Tom Browkaw's *The Greatest Generation* in 2000 has fueled additional interest in the personal histories of men and women who served in the Second World War. Literally hundreds of histories of the war exist, and hundreds more photo journalistic accounts have been published since 1945, such as Life Magazine's *Picture History of World War II,* or *The American Heritage History of World War II.* Both of these genres have provided the reading public with images and narrative histories of this conflict, and they have been more recently accompanied by televised accounts such as *The World at War,* originally produced by the BBC and shown also on American television. The historian, Stephen Ambrose, has done much to focus our attention on the Second World War as an event of American history in his writing an important narrative account of June 6, 1944 and in his development of a museum in New Orleans devoted to the military events of that period. (New Orleans is where the famous "Higgins Boats," those landing craft used in the Normandy and other amphibious invasions, were mass produced before "the longest day.") The Ambrose contributions to our understanding of the war also include tours of Normandy and other European battlefields, just as the Civil War historian James McPherson has developed excursions to the sites of Civil War conflicts. But both McPherson and Ambrose have recently focused attention on the experience of these wars by examining the testimonies of small groups of common soldiers, even individual histories, as a way of understanding the larger conflict. This is "social history" at its best, the study of the human experience from the "bottom up" rather than from the "top down." The Ambrose book about the Battle of the Bulge, for example, follows the intimate, daily experience of members of the Third Army as they advanced toward and then defended Bastogne, and it is called simply, *Band of Brothers*. The television documentary that was based on this book is also called "Band of Brothers," but the video version also contains interviews with living members of the "band of brothers" who are represented by actors in the visual account. These interviews add veracity to the visual text and develop a more personalized approach to historical narration. Both of these accounts, the written and the visual drama, introduce the reader/viewer to a post-war genre of writing known as "literary journalism." Practitioners of the craft of literary journalism are faced with a tremendous challenge, to develop compelling narratives from real human events while relating those events as truthfully as possible. Earlier, the nineteenth-century novelist Stephen Crane composed a very realistic account of the Civil War in *The Red Badge of Courage*. This is also "literary journalism", loosely conceived, because Crane was not a veteran of the Civil War, having been born in 1871, well after the war had ended.

One feature of literary journalism now widely acknowledged is that the personal testimonies of participants in a significant event of history, such as the September 11, 2001, tragedy at the World Trade Centers in New York City, can, on reflection, develop a composite narrative of that day that will offer unusual insight unavailable from any other source. This does not mean that "social history" becomes the compilation of accounts gathered in the street rather than in the library archives; rather, it means that historians are now giving more value than ever to the accounts of participants in an historical moment. These local voices provide a perspective and add a dimension to the larger construction of a historical landscape that no scholar working alone in a library or archive can possibly achieve.

Amherst Rotary Goes to War is just such an historical document. This general introduction frames the personal accounts of some Amherst Rotarians who still attend meetings and who were active participants in the Second World War. These accounts are not arranged chronologically or topically; rather, they appear alphabetically so that the reader can come to know the participant from his own words rather than from the excerpts a historian might select and edit from a larger account. Some of these accounts have been selected from much longer narratives by the same authors. For example, former Amherst Town Manager Allen Torrey authored *Flight Time: 1943-47* in 2000; this has been edited and photographs selected for inclusion here. Similarly, Frank Chapman, who flew the PanAm Clipper with President Franklin Roosevelt returning from the Casablanca conference authored *Talking to the World: from PanAm's Clippers* in 1999. Both the Torrey and Chapman texts have been edited, as has the forthcoming autobiography of Duncan Fraser, one of the Normandy veterans who wrote the story of his life. Some of the following accounts are reproduced verbatim and were brief enough to be included without significant editing. However, the important rule followed throughout the editorial process was that the voice of the participant was to be preserved as much as possible, and the spirit of his narrative should also be preserved. Thus the veracity of each account and the narrative voice of each testimony should take precedence over any attempt to offer a historian's account of these events of the Second World War. In the spirit of the social historian's concern for the testimony of participants in history, *Amherst Rotary Goes to War* seeks to give voice to each of those veterans of the conflict we have been so fortunate to know in our years as Amherst Rotarians.

Finally, we must explain the absence of women's voices from this volume. While Rotary International now appropriately has many women members, like many colleges and universities, it has only in the past few decades gone co-ed, and most of the women members are too young to have served in the Second World War. In conclusion, while this volume celebrates the participation, even the heroism, of some veterans of World War II, we were all reminded, in 1995, of a different viewpoint, when Gerry Grady, USMC, Rotary member and participant in the invasion of Okinawa, concluded his oral presentation with an appreciation for our interest in his war experience but with a stern reminder that "there is nothing remotely romantic about it. All war is hell." This echo of William Tecumseh Sherman's observation that "war is hell"(1880), is as true today as it was then and as it was in Grady's experience at Okinawa. These personal testimonies may also be viewed as memorials to the fallen comrades of these Amherst veterans who did not return, as they have, to live full lives in the United States, and it is to those fallen soldiers that this volume is respectfully dedicated.

Amherst Rotarians who Served in World War II not represented in the book include the following names. A full list of Amherst veterans of the Second World War may be found in the Jones Library, Amity Street, Amherst, Massachusetts. In addition, the Amherst Rotary Club archives, also housed there, contains several tape recordings of Amherst Rotary WWII veterans, e.g., Tom Carhart and Frank Chapman. Each is about two hours and supplements the information found in the testimonials that follow here.

Edward "Andy" Anderson	Harold Elder	Jerome Peterson
Theodore S. Bacon	A. J. Donald Hastings	Phillip F. Reneaud
Roy R. Blair	Robert D. Hawley	Everett L. Roberts
Bruce G. Brown	Horace W. Hewlett	Frederick G. Ruder, Jr.
William G. Colby	Robert S. Hopkins	Henry A. Tadgell
William Cole	Joseph D. Mascis	William Tunis
Kenneth D. Cuddeback	George May	Everett C. Warner
R. Harlow Cutting	Warren P. McGurik	Stanley Ziomek
	Hamilton I. Newell	

TESTIMONY OF THE REV. JOHN BALCOM

Rank: A.B. Seaman, United States Coast Guard Division I, Cape Cod Canal, Massachusetts, and Ketchikan, Alaska 1942-43. Every weekend was spent at the State Pier, buzzard's Bay, Massachusetts

We were guarding the Cape Cod Canal property and logging ships and convoys passing through the canal, many with damages from German submarines. We were also escorting pilots to convoys in our Coast Guard boats and tending to the submarine nets off Cape Cod, designed to trap enemy submarines.

1944-45. I was attached to Ketchikan, Alaska, Coast Guard Station, mapping the Yukon River from headquarters at Fort Yukon. We provided hospitality for pilots and counseling at the Air Base at Tanacross, Alaska, one of the stops for the P-38s being ferried to Fairbanks for Russian pilots who were allies flying our USAAF aircraft. The photograph below was made during this period.

THOMAS CARHART, USAAF

On June 30, 2003, Tom Carhart was interviewed by Mason Lowance and Allen Torrey in his home at the Arbors, University Drive, Amherst, Massachusetts. What follows is a summary of that two hour interview, which was tape recorded and is available as part of the Amherst Rotary archive in the Jones Library, Amherst, Massachusetts. Colonel Carhart is an extremely distinguished aviator, having remained in the military service after the end of World War II, flying everything from Stearman biplanes to F-104 Phantom Jet fighter-bombers. During World War II, he was stationed primarily in the European Theater, flying the P-38 and P51 fighters as escort for bombing raids over Germany. His initial training was as an infantry officer, USA, and he was attached to an infantry unit on December 16, 1941. Temporary assignments in California and Hawaii led eventually to flight training as an infantry officer, USAAF, and on December 5, 1943, Carhart received his commission and wings, and was assigned to the 44e Fighter Squadron. His first aircraft after training was the P-39, a single engine fighter that carried two 50mm machine guns in the wings and one 20mm cannon mounted in the propeller shaft. He also flew the P-63 and P-38, a twin-tail extremely fast and maneuverable fighter in which he became a flight instructor, training other pilots at Williams AFB, Phoenix, Arizona, a post he occupied from six months to one year following commission.

*Colonel Tom Carhart commenced as an infantryman in
the U.S. Army. He is pictured here with his Springfield
rifle in 1936 in infantry fatigues. The picture below
is in full USAF uniform, highly decorated.*

Carhart's European tour commenced in January, 1945, when he made a six thousand mile voyage from Santa Rosa, California, to Naples, Italy, in thirty days. He was assigned to the 97`" Fighter Squadron, 82nd Fighter Group, USAAF. He was based primarily in Foggia, Italy, and flew missions escorting bombers over Germany and occupied Europe. The era of the aerial "dogfight" had occurred earlier in the war, largely over England during the `Battle of Britain" in 1940. Carhart's squadron focused on air-to-ground attack, specifically against bridges, railroad depots, and other "targets of opportunity." On one occasion, he was chased by the newly developed German ME 262, a jet powered fighter-bomber, but managed to evade the attacker and avoid aerial combat with this much faster aircraft. On another occasion, his P-38 was armed with two 500 pound bombs, one of which Carhart was able to put down the smokestack of a munitions factory, which instantly imploded on explosion and impact from the bomb.

Following the war, Carhart remained in the USAAF but was assigned to the Pentagon, doing Air Force publicity and procurement. He maintained his flight status throughout the years 1945-1950 by flying everything from propeller driven aircraft that had been developed at the end of the war, such as the P-51 "Mustang", to the recently introduced jets, such as the T-33. His beloved P-38s in which he had flown successful missions during the last years of World War II were phased out in favor of the faster and more powerful, better armed P-51, an,(aircraft that saw combat duty during the Korean war. Carhart had also flown the P-47 "Thunderbolt", one of the heaviest but most powerful combat aircraft of the Second World War. [During the taped interview, Allen Torrey mentioned that he had also flown the P-47 several times, even though his primary aircraft assignment was the C-47, a twin-engine cargo and personnel transport. Carhart said that he had "checked out" as co-pilot on the C-47, even though his primary assignments were to single-engine, fighter aircraft. He flew C-47s for several years out of Orly Field, outside Paris, France, during and just after the Korean War.]

Assigned to Maxwell Field in Selma, Alabama, Carhart saw the transformation of the air wing of the U.S. Army into the United

States Air Force in the years following World War II. He logged many hours in the T-33, a two-seat fighter trainer in which he was also an instructor. As noted above, he also was assigned to Orly Field, near Paris, France, for several years, during which he flew the C-47 transport as well as the single-engine fighters and trainers for jet pilots. One of the most thrilling aircraft he flew was the F-4 Phantom jet fighter-bomber, which had a payload of bombs exceeding that of the B-17 four engine aircraft of the USAAF during World War II. During the interview, Carhart acknowledged fear when he pushed this plane to "Mach H and slightly beyond," some two times the speed of sound(750 miles per hour, or above 1500 miles per hour). But he carries a Tattoo of the P-38, perhaps his most beloved aircraft. Still, if he had to engage the enemy today, he would prefer the faster, more powerful, better armed jet fighters.

Thomas Carhart and Allen Torrey in Carhart's hot-air baloon, which he flew over the Pioneer Valley many times after his retirement from the United States Air Force. Courageous passengers were treated to half-hour or more rides over Amherst and neighboring towns, from which the landscape below was spectacular. Flights usually got under way early, commencing about five or six in the morning.

The P-38 Lightning

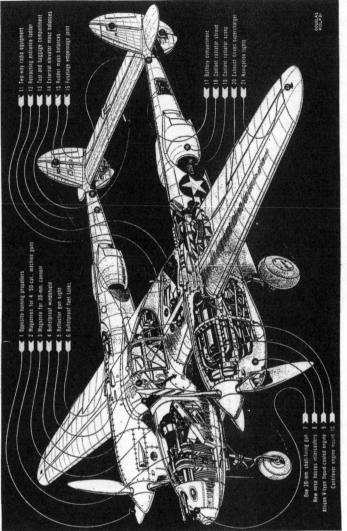

Army Air Forces Twin-Engine Fighter (World War II)

The Lockheed P-38 Lightning had a wingspan of 52 feet, and a length of 37 feet, 10 inches, with an overall height of 11 feet, 6 inches. Speed was "well over 400 mph" and she could reach an altitude of eight miles. In combat, the P-38's wing flaps were extended to tighten turns. The plane cost $125,000.

(Lockheed drawing)

FRANK CHAPMAN TESTIMONY

THE NAVY CALLS

People used to ask me what I did during World War II. I suspect that my answer was usually sort of vague. As you know I flew for PAA from 1939 until 1949 and remained on their payroll all during that period. At the time we didn't know what was going to happen because the draft board had started calling some of Trippe's precious flight crews to active duty. And he certainly wouldn't permit that he said.

I later found out that there had been many meetings between Trippe, the War Dept. and Franklin D. Roosevelt, as to what to do with the "Chosen Instrument" as Pan Am was referred to. After much heated discussion a consensus was reached. The PAA flight crews would be taken into the Naval Air Transport Service (NATS) and therefore the flight crews would remain intact. Trippe and we were happy about that arrangement.

At the time we were told very little as to just what was happening. But one day in May we were told to report to the Navy enlistment center at Grand Central Railroad Station in New York. When we arrived in the city to register along with thousands of other young guys, we sat and fidgeted, wondering what was next.

With continuous announcements over the PA system and lots of signs we crept along from area to area. We went through all the usual military paper work, then stood naked in line while we waited for our physicals (quite a scene) followed by more waiting with everybody asking everyone else questions as to what did we expect would happen and when. Most everyone agreed that we would be aboard a train before nightfall headed for the Great Lakes training center somewhere in Michigan. We spent all day in this process.

Every few minutes the PA system announced that still another numbered group should report to track number so and so and climb aboard. The massive group of young men that had arrived earlier was steadily diminishing and we still hadn't been called with a track number. Finally, along about dinner time a cryptic announcement was given, "all aviation flight crew members return to your company offices immediately". We collectively breathed a sigh of relief, as we realized we could sleep at home one more night. So our group quickly rushed around getting onto subways, trains or whatever, to get out of there before the Navy changed its mind.

As I sat on the Long Island Rail Road, I pondered what would happen to me next. All I knew at that point was that I was officially in the Navy, but I didn't have a clue just what that meant except that my rank was now Aviation Chief Radioman. Some of the crew were given Lieutenant JG, if they had a college degree. The flight engineer was ranked as an Aviation Chief Mechanic. The skippers were either Lt. or Lt. Commander, if they had Navy time.

The Navy had already delivered several of their sea planes to PAA and I was checked out right away because of my high seniority. That's how I got to stay home waiting for Ken to arrive. For my own reference the U. S. Navy amphibian aircraft I was checked out on were N7083, N7086 and N7087.

I believe I was one of the first to check out on the newly delivered Navy planes. Their radio gear and Loran were great. So I got to fly around and around New England while a group of pilots checked out on the Navy PB2Y3 Consolidated Coronado four engined amphibian. During these flights Captain Harold Gray checked out Captains Gulbransen and Delima. The FROs I checked out included DR, SM, FM AND GC all newly trained FROs who aren't on my old list.

Just before my first official flight for the Navy, I had been issued khaki and olive drab uniforms, that at a distance looked like a Naval uniform but they were slightly different. I liked the olive drab one the best.

On Sept 12, 1943, we left La Guardia Bay aboard the N7087 with Capt. Mitchell bound for Fort de France via Bermuda and returned via San Juan and Bermuda. Those babies were extremely noisy as there was no sound proofing and poor heating. But the radio gear was certainly better than we had on the Clippers. It also had advanced navigational equipment such as LORAN, Long range navigation. Loran would give very accurate position fixes in a few minutes with no difficult calculations and no learning curve. Anyone could learn to use the system in minutes. The r/t flight time was 25:15 minutes.

We carried a load of mysterious crates, boxes and packages that no one took time to say what the stuff was. Even the Navy personnel were of course close mouthed about who they were or where they were headed. Needless to say, we were kind of curious but essentially found out nothing. Do any of you remember the war saying "Loose lips sinks ships"? That is what everyone was trying not to do. Name, rank and serial number was supposed to be the extent of what they would say about themselves. Those Navy planes were all painted dull sea gray as were PAA `s nine Boeing B-314s.

The Boeing interior had also drastically been changed. The berths, some floor- ing and other unnecessary or luxury passenger comforts were removed to make space for more cargo and the age of shut-ding had begun. Joe Hart, one of the skippers, crossed the Atlantic 12 times in 13 days. I commonly had five round trips across the South Atlantic between Natal and Fish Lake, plus a couple of trips to Lisbon from Fish Lake all in 30 days.

Essentially we carried priority passengers and cargo on both the B-314 and the PB2Y3s. The only real difference was that on the Navy flights, we often went into Naval bases some of which were supposed to be real secret especially Lough Neigh in northwest Ireland where we flew military VIPs into late at night. Also on the South Atlantic flights we'd stop at a Navy base, Port Lyautey in Morocco.

We flew Admirals, Generals, Kings and Queens like King George of Greece and Queen Wilhelmina of the Netherlands, lots of USO groups including film stars such as Bob Hope, Francis Langford,

Jerry Colonna, Martha Raye and Carmen Miranda. I was on board when we took that particular group to North Africa in 1943 via the South Atlantic and into Fish Lake where connections were made with Army flights.

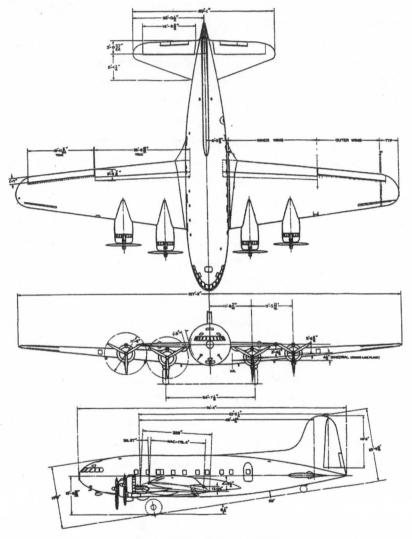

Three View of Boeing 307

One night flight across the mid Atlantic we had Clare Booth Luce as a passenger. She was the writer and wife of the Time Life publisher. The couple of times I passed her bunk in the middle of the night I could hear the click, dick of her typewriter behind the night curtains. She wrote about her flight "Fifty years from now, people will look back on a Clipper flight of today as the most romantic voyage of history"

And I agreed with her completely. Despite the stress, sweat, sleepiness and fear there was a romance about each flight. It seems a bit hard to explain to those who had not experienced it. But it was most always fun too. Each closely knit crew were all professionals in their own field but we all enjoyed a joke or two to lighten up a tiring long flight.

Sometime during the summer of 1943 our crew had a four day layover in Lisbon waiting for the next inbound flight from New York. We had flown in from the Azores the night before. Pan Am billeted us at the former royal palace of Prince Don Carlos, son of the King of Portugal. It had been renamed the Aviz Hotel. It was truly a spectacularly furnished place on the beautiful broad Aveneda Liberdade, in downtown Lisbon.

It must have been noon when several of us had finally risen. We were all hungry so agreed to get coffee and a sandwich at one of the many lovely sidewalk cafes in the middle of the wide and busy Aveneda. The downtown Lisbon area had gorgeous flower gardens that bloomed most of the year. It was sunny and romantic, as we sat and absorbed the warm sunshine. After ordering we slid into our usual custom of girl watching.

At lunchtime these broad Avenedas with their artistic mosaic sidewalks, were crowded with pretty senoritas slowly sauntering past us. As they passed, some would give us sly smiles others a big grin. They knew we young Americans were watching their every movement. Some had real bouncy steps.

I sat with Jake our Flight Engineer. He had a slight hazy stare that began to form as a particularly attractive young lady glided past. We both looked at each other and began nodding our heads and grinning. We enthusiastically agreed that she was stunning. Her physical attributes rang our bells.

Now Jake was one of those men who liked technical things especially math. He'd sit in front of the Flight Engineer's instrument panel of gauges and switches and doodle with numbers. He designed formulas to solve his flight problems. He carried a small plastic pocket slide rule (before computers) to work out a problem. We watched him solve the pounds of fuel remaining on board. This was always the question. Did we have enough fuel to our destination plus one hour to spare. I knew an idea was forming as we sipped the great strong coffee. He whipped out his slide rule and wet his stubby pencil tip with his tongue. He put down some numbers on a paper napkin.

He suggested we get serious about rating the swarms of young lovelies passing us. So we decided we'd try rating them by the mammary movement (MM) or M2. It would be a beat system calculated on each two steps they took. Then we began to add other factors because it seemed more complicated then we first thought.

Jake did a series of calculations on mass versus diameter versus density and time. Then he tried to estimate total volume that would be needed to fill say a 36B cup bra and on to a 38D cup. After filling a couple of pages in his pocket note book with numbers, he decided that a 36C could be the norm. Here's how he figured it out. The breast would bounce upward on the first step and immediately drop down. On the next step, the other half of the cycle would be completed, identical to the first step. This kind of bouncy breast movement, he avered, would be rated as a two beater.

We two eager young 28 year old male chauvinist pigs (MCP) with nothing more important to do at that moment tried out the system. We very soon found out that there were many variables that we'd not taken into consideration. For instance:

A. **Length of stride.**
B. **Steps per minute ie casual, moderate or in a big hurry.**
C. **Body weight and height.**
D. **Bra and cup size.**
E. **Bra material: durable cotton, sheer netting or neither.**
F. **Blouse material, button location and fit.**

Jake and I dedicated over an hour on this fascinating session until the crowds began to thin. Our initial findings were that the absolutely best and most sensational rating was a 2 1/2 beater. Thee topped the list and we saw several during this first test observation.

This silly pastime of ours seemed to catch on quickly by word of mouth. It wasn't long before other Lisbon layover crews were sitting having a leisure lunch in their own cafe observation posts as they busily eyeballed the busty beauties as they passed.

We soon ran into a problem on some of our later observation sessions. And we weren't able to make an accurate rating on one particular type of lovely lady. If we saw she was braless and in a hurry our rating system went out the window. The multiple movements of the mammary mass messed our minds and confused our senses. We just had to rate those as 2-112 plus!

So this commentary is a moments glance into old time flight crew history as to how we exhausted flyboys spent time resting and recreating R and R Many other flyboys were much more active as you may have read about in the past. Those more romantic escapades between a few handsome single. Captains and Pan Am's delightful Stewardesses. They were legend but that's not my story here.

By present day 1990's standards of feminine ethics, we old MCP's were looking at those lovely Lisbon ladies as sex objects. I now know that was wrong and I apologize to the modern feminist for my bold and thoughtless statements of yore, "them were the facts Ms". I've tried to modify my present day behavior and have tried not to play that game any more. (At least I don't say the ratings out loud any more.)

PAA FLIES FDR TO CASABLANCA

Probably what later became a very well known and famous flight started out in early 1943 as an ultra secret flight which was designated as special mission #71.

The Navy secretly arranged with the New York Atlantic Division manager Leslie for two B-314s to be in Miami with the usual double crew. When the first Boeing docked at Dinner Key in Miami, they were told to standby for a passenger "Mr. Jones" and leave immediately, as soon as he was on board.

The mysterious passenger "Mr. Jones" fully cloaked and in a wheel chair was lifted aboard, followed by a small group that appeared to be carefully protecting the wheel chaired passenger. The crew immediately recognized their passenger as President Roosevelt. They were shocked and surprised as no one had been told about this especially important VIP. Leslie had told no one, not even Trippe.

What was later reported, Capt. Cone had been handed a sealed envelope when he left La Guardia, N. Y. and told to open it only after passengers had been boarded in Miami. On opening the envelope, it confirmed that FDR was indeed aboard, and that they were to fly him to Fishermans Lake. He'd then be driven a few miles to the Monrovia airport where the Army Air Force would transport him to Casablanca for a conference with Prime Minister Churchill and Stalin.

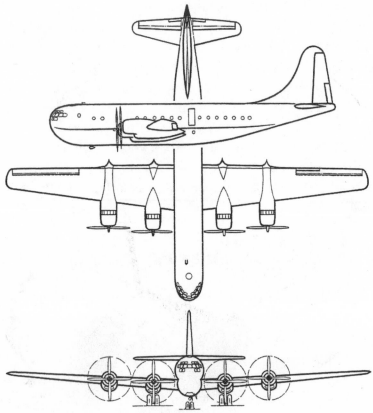

Three View of Boeing 377 Stratocruiser

On FDR's return flight the Clipper met him at Fishermans i,ake. On that night flight somewhere over the South Atlantic, he celebrated his 61st birthday with a cake decorated by one of the stewards. According to Harry Hopkins, FDR enjoyed his flight tremendously as it was the first time he had been able to fly since taking office. When the flight crossed the equator he was initiated into the "Short Snorters Club".

A bit of personal background on this famous flight. For once my memory is a bit fuzzy on these details but I thought I had been as-signed to the second, decoy flight that was to takeoff from Miami 30 minutes ahead of the plane that "Mr. Jones" was on. At the last minute, I was replaced by Stan Call and I never knew why. The reason I have mentioned this was that I had been the acting Chief FRO when Chief Harry Drake was needed elsewhere. So I had been privy to the very briefest of details on this hush-hush trip . My best guess on why my memory seems fuzzy was that probably Division Manager Leslie had told me to handle the communications details for the two flights, take care of them and then destroy anything written and forget all the rest. Someone above me may have shifted the whole flight crew at the last minute to prevent any possible leaks about the flight. Who knows?

Testimony of Frank Chapman, United States Navy and Pan American Clipper Radio Operator Officer

Hadley, MA 01035
June 21, 2003

Dear Mason:

I flew with Pan Am from 1939 to 1949 as a Flight Radio Officer and Navigator. Pan Am had a contract with the Navy from 1944 to 1946. During that time I flew aboard the PB2Y3 amphibian across the Atlantic to Lisbon via Bermuda, Azores and Lisbon. I had over 500 flight hours with the Navy.

My rating in the Naval Aviation Transport System was Aviation Chief Radioman, Class SV6, USNR 907-46-60. As a Pan Am Flight Radio Officer, I flew under contract with NATS for two years from 1944 to 1946. I was trained aboard the PB2Y3 and my shake down flight was to Fort de France via Bermuda and San Juan. I was based at La Guardia and assigned to fly anywhere the Navy had needs. I fle numerous night flight across the Atlantic to such secret navy bases such as Loch Neigh, Ireland and Port Lyautey, Morocco and others. We were told before each flight that we were not to discuss anything about our flight plans, nor who was aboard or what cargo we were carrying. Cameras were not allowed anywhere around the aircraft so we couldn't take photos. This was to protect the rules of secrecy during the war so we never had any photos. Our theater of operations was Europe and Africa.

I received an Honorable Discharge from the Navy on Feb. 1, 1946.

Johnny Willmott, an old Flight Radio Officer friend located the attached photos of the PB2Y3. He flew with the Navy just before WW2 began so the security was not as important.

Author Francis Allan Chapman, FRO.
Photo PAA, Pan Am Historical Foundation

High Flight

Oh, I have slipped the surly bonds of earth
    And danced the skies on laughter-silvered wings.
Sunward I've climbed, and joined the tumbling mirth
    Of sun-split clouds—and done a hundred things.
You have not dreamed of—wheeled and soared and swung,
    High in the sunlit silence. Hov'cing there,
I've chased the shouting wind along, and flung
    My eager craft through footless halls of air.
Up, up, the long, delirious, burning blue
    I've topped the windswept heights with easy grace.
Where never a lark, or even an eagle flew
    And, whilst with silent, lifting mind I've trod
The high untrespassed sanctity of space,
    Put out my hand, and touched the face of GOD.

John Gillespie Magee Jr
(1922-1941)

The Martin Company

Four of these handsome Martin Mars JRM lying boats were used by Naval Air Transport Service between 1946 and 1956 for personnel and freight carrying between California and Hawaii. During these ten years they made hundreds of round trips, and piled up better than 75,000 hours of flying time in an operation which, according to a report made on August 9, 1955, by Rear Admiral James S. Russell, then Chief of the Bureau of -Aeronautics, "compared favorably cost-wise with its landplane competition of the same vintage: the Douglas DC-4 and Skymaster," and, in fact, "was more economical to operate by 28% than the Skymaster on the same route.

During their decade of service, the four JRMs were the world's largest operational flying boats in active military service. The Caroline Mars established a world's non-stop flight record for seaplanes on a 4748 mile flight from Honolulu direct to Chicago on August 27, 1948, with a payload of 14,049 pounds and 42 persons aboard. A sister ship, Marshall Mars, which was destroyed by fire in 1950, achieved a world's record for the number of passengers carried on a single flight by transporting 301 men and a seven man crew from San Diego to Alameda on May 19, 1949. Each of the Mars boats remained in the water for six to eight months at a time.

With Pratt & Whitney 4360-4T engines, the Mars cruised at 215 miles per hour while grossing 165,000 pounds, more than twice that of the Boeing Clipper. (Payload was 30,000 pounds.)

One and possibly two Mars boats remain in service to this day as forest fire fighters in British Columbia.

PAA "Capetown Clipper", NC 18612, Foynes 1944

My roommates Oscar Olson and Charlie Chase,
Dinner Key, Florida, during our preparations for overseas
transport via PAA Clippers during World War II

The S-38 carried eight passengers at 105 MPH, fast for its day, with a range of 300 miles. It had a two man crew, the FRO sat the right seat. This is a sister plane flown by the author to Merida_ Note that no flien instruments visible. FRO sent his UW radio messages with the code key clipped to his knee. He also served the famous FAA cold chicken box lunches to passengers. After landing, he picked up the buoy line when Skipper got dose enough to reach. Pan Am Historical. Foundation, University of Miami, Richter Library

Early model Pan American radio regeneration receiver model ACC, serial #56. Believe the front panel hinged outward to change inductance coils to cover different aircraft frequencies. Believe it went with the FAA 10F3 transmitter with about 10/ 15 watts output. FRO Chapman believes these were the models they had to tear down and rebuild during training at Dinner Key. Ralph Conly

*Flight radio operating station - includes 2 transmitters,
2 receivers & Loran navigational system. 1943*

*Aircraft of the type used by Chapman's PAA crew to fly President
Franklin Delano Roosevelt to and from Casablanca, 1943*

Boeing 307, "Flying Cloud," NC19903. Photo showing Mr. and Mrs. Frank Chapman ready to go take off from Miami airport to Rio de Janerio, leaving for a long foreign assignment. The trip took five days, and covered 5400 miles. High altitude for "Flying Cloud" was 30,000 feet but cabin pressure was comfortable at 5,000 feet. This picture was made August 27, 1940, in Miami, Florida

"Mr. Jones" (President Roosevelt) aboard a B314 Clipper enroute to Casablanca summit with Churchill. He enjoyed his 61st birthday somewhere over the South Atlantic between Natal, Brazil and Fisherman's Lake. His aides were Admiral Leahy and Harry Hopkins with PAA Captain Howard Cone right foreground. This was an ultra secret special flight #71, 1943. P. Am Historical Foundation

Frank Chapman at Rotary picnic, 2003, with Allen Torrey

C3. 4052   Series C

Honorable Discharge

from the

United States Navy

This is to certify that

FRANCIS ALLEN CHAPMAN   *a* Aviation Chief Radioman (AA),
                                         Class SV-6, USNR, 907 46 60

is **Honorably Discharged** *from the* Headquarters Third Naval District

New York, N.Y.   *and from the Naval Service of the United States*

this 1st *day of* February 1946

This certificate is awarded as a Testimonial of Fidelity and Obedience.

B. D. ROLSTON, Lt., USNR
By direction of ComTHREE

Pan American Airways
Boeing 314 Clipper

The Boeing 314 Clipper was designed to meet a Pan American specification for a flying boat capable of carrying upward of 75 passengers and a crew of six to ten on long trans-ocean hops, something the Martin M-130 could not manage to do.

By early 1939 six had entered service, four on the North Atlantic run and two in the Pacific, and Pan American contracted with Boeing for half a dozen more. Of the latter, the British Government purchased three, while the others were operated by Pan American for the U. S. Navy.

Like all big flying boats, the passengers rode in a degree of great comfort. The hull of the Clipper, far larger than the fuselage of any land plane of the day, was so spacious that passengers rattled around in it like peas in a pod. It was divided into two decks: the top contained the control room, cargo space and crew quarters; the lower was divided into seven 10-passenger compartments.

It was powered by four 1600 horsepower Wright twin Cyclones, all of which could be reached in flight via a tunnel in the wing. These produced a top speed of 199 miles per hour and a cruise of 184, with maximum range extending to 5200 miles.

The last of the great Clippers ended its days in mid _Atlantic some years after the war, following a forced landing after passing its point of no return. Bermuda Sky Queen, operated by a non-scheduled carrier and bound for New York from Europe with 80-odd passengers aboard, landed in high seas. Thanks to the fine seamanship of the rescuing Coast Guard and the boat's superb seaworthiness, not a person was lost. The Clipper, however, its nose bashed in from contact with the rescuing cutter but otherwise not seriously damaged, was sunk by the rescuers as a menace to navigation.

*"**PB2Y3:** In response to reports from the war in Europe, the armament and horsepower were increased and self-sealing fuel tanks installed.*
Crew: *10 Power Plant Four 1,200 hp Pratt & Whitney R-1830-88*
Weight: *Empty 40,935 lbs Gross 68,000 lbs Fuel: 2893 gals. internal; 1509 gals. aux.*
Dimensions: *Wing area 1,780 sq ft Wing span 115 ft Length 79 ft 3 in Height 27 ft 6 in*
Armament: *Eight 50-caliber flexible machine guns Up to four 1,000 lb bombs external and eight 1,000 lb bombs internal*
Performance: *@ 66,000 lbs. Max Speed: 213 kts. @ 20,000 ft.*
Stall Speed: *75 kts. (power on). Rate of Climb: 580 fpm. Time to Climb: 21.8 min. to 10,000 ft. Range: 2,930 nm @ 135 kts. @ 2,500 ft. Service Ceiling 21,300 ft.*
PB2Y-3R: *The turrets were removed and faired over and other modifications were made to convert the aircraft to a transport configuration." End of my copy.*

PERFORMANCE DATA ON AIRCRAFT FLOWN BY AUTHOR

	Sikorsky S-38A	Sikorsky S-38B	Cons. Commodore	Sikorsky S-40	Sikorsky S40-A	Sikorsky S-2	Sikorsky S-42A	Sikorsky S-42B	Sikorsky S-43			
Type	Amphibian	Amphibian	Boat	Amphibian	Amphibian	Boat	Boat	Boat	Amphibian	Boat	Boat	Boat
Length	40 ft.	40 ft.	68 ft.	77 ft.	77 ft.	68 ft.	68 ft.	68 ft.	51 ft.	90 ft.	106 ft.	106 ft.
Span	72 ft.	72 ft.	100 ft.	114 ft.	114 ft.	114 ft.	118 ft.	118 ft.	86 ft.	130 ft.`	152 ft.	152 ft.
Wing Loading						28.5 lb/sq. ft.	29.9 lbs/sq.ft	31.3 lbs/sq. ft.	25 lbs/sq. ft.			
Height	14 ft.	14 ft.	16 ft.	24 ft.	24 ft.	17 ft.	17 ft.	17 ft.	18 ft.	25 ft.	28 ft.	28 ft.
Gross weight	9,200 lbs.	9,900 lbs.	17,650 lbs.	34,010 lbs.	34,600 lbs.	38,000 lbs.	40,000 lbs.	42,000 lbs.	20,000 lbs.	51,000 lbs.+	82,000 lbs.	84,000 lbs.
Engines	P&W WaspX2	P&W HornetX2	P&W Hornet X2	P&W Hornet BX4	P&W Hornet T2DIX4	P&W Hornet X 4	P&W Hornet X2	P&W Hornet X4	P&W Hornet X2	P&W Twin Wasp X4	Wright Cyclone X4	Wright Cyclone X4
Horsepower	410	450	575hp	575hp	660hp	700 hp	750 hp	750 hp	750 hp	800 hp (later 800hp)	1500 hp	1600 hp
Range	595 statute mi.	595 statute mi.	1,000 statute mi.	800 mi.	800 mi.	1,200 mi.	1,200 mi.	1,200 mi.	775 statute mi.	3000 pass 4000 mail only	3,500 statute mi.s	4,275 statute mi.
Fuel capacity	330 gal.	330 gal.	650 gal.	1040 gal.	1,060 gal.	1,240 gal.	1,240 gal.	1,240 gal.	690 gal.	4,000 gal.	4,200 gal.	5,448 gal.
Useful load	9,900 lbs.	9,900 lbs.		10,870 lbs.	11,400 lbs.	18,000 lbs.	18,000 lbs.	18,000 lbs.				
Cruising speed	112 mph	110 mph	102 mph	115 mph	120 mph	150 mph	160 mph	155 mph	166 mph	22,784 lbs. 157 mph	23,500 lbs. 150 mph	31,360 lbs. 150 mph
Service ceiling	20,000 ft. min.	19,000 ft. min.	10,000 ft.	13,000 ft.	12,500 ft.	16,000 ft.	20,000 ft.	15,000 ft.	19,000 ft.	20,000 ft.	21,000 ft.	21,000 ft.
Climb rate	940 ft./min.	880 ft./min.		712 ft./min.	712 ft./min.	800 ft./min.	800 ft./min.	800 ft./min.	1,000 ft./min.	800 ft./min.		
Passengers	8	8	22	34	40	38	38	24	16/18	43 (as sleeper 18)	74 (34 at night)	74 (34 at night)
Crew	3	3	4	5	6	5	5	5	3	7	10-16	10-16

EARLY SEAPLANES FLOWN BY FRANK CHAPMAN, BEGINNING IN 1930S

Pan American World Airways

In May 1928, Igor Sikorsky, then a struggling designer and builder working in an unheated, leaky hangar at Roosevelt Field, completed his first amphibian — the S-38 — the prototype of a succession of highly successful planes to follow. Production of the S-38 continued on into 1930 with over a hundred constructed. It was hardly a handsome plane, its hull suspended beneath a high wing, its tail surfaces attached by outriggers, but it was a fine performer. With its twin 425 horsepower Wasps, it cruised at 124 miles per hour, climbed 880 feet per minute and could take off from still water in 16 seconds. Level flight could be maintained on either engine. It was wet on takeoff, particularly in a wind, its low-slung props blasting spray back across its hull and windshield, obliterating its pilot's vision until it reached planing speed.

Sikorsky Aircraft, Div, Of United Aircraft

The Sikorsky S-39, a 5-place amphibian created for the sportsman pilot late in 1929. Powered by a single Pratt & Whitney Wasp Jr. (300-420 horsepower) the S-39 proved itself in various operations including commercial passenger carrying, African exploration — even as an aerial yacht tender. PanAm loaned both models to Navy (1944-1946)

JOHN T. CONLON

Born: October 27, 1923
Army Serial Number: 31261966
Rank: Staff Sergeant, U. S. Army Air Force

IN THE BEGINNING...

At the time of my induction into the Armed services on March 30, 1943 at Fort Devens, Massachusetts, I was given the opportunity to express a preference as to which branch of military service I wished to be assigned. Luck was with me, in that after requesting the Army Air Force, I was given the choice I had indicated. Immediately there-upon, I was assigned for basic training for a four-week period at Air Force facilities in Atlantic City, New Jersey.

Upon completion of basic training, I was transferred to a military installation at the former Pawling School in Pawling, New York for a four-week training period as a Cryptographer. At this ultra-secure, heavily guarded location no one in our group was allowed to leave the premises during the entire period of our instruction in and practice with the secret codes and ciphers used by the U.S. Military. To say the least, this turned out an extremely intensive and confining experience for all involved in that program. At the same time, however, it also is true that the pressures and isolation that accompanied our training forged bonds of friendship and respect among the members of our small group which lasted throughout the remainder of our military service.

Following graduation from that program, I was assigned to Seymour Johnson Field in Goldsboro, North Carolina for an approximately one month period of overseas training. Thereafter, I was transferred for the purpose of embarkation overseas first to Camp Patrick Henry adjacent to the port of Newport News, Virginia and then later to Camp Shanks, a few miles up the Hudson River from the port of New York, New York to await boarding a troop transport vessel.

EMBARKATION

On a Sunday morning mid September 1943 a substantial contingent of servicemen from all branches of the military ferried down the Hudson River to board a vast fleet of large ships docked in New York Harbor. Somewhat strangely (to be explained later), it was my good fortune to be among those who boarded the Empress of Russia, an ancient and weary British Merchant Marine former passenger liner. Later that afternoon we departed the dock, and then the harbor itself, and later began to join a massive convoy assembling off Long Island in heavy fog and growing dusk. Standing by the railing watching all those ships approach though the haze was an exciting and somewhat somber experience, for none of us on board had the slightest notion of what part of the world we were heading toward.. However, at luck would have it, our ship became disabled overnight, and two destroyers escorted us back into New York Harbor. One week to the day later, our group, still intact, boarded the modern and speedy French liner Mauritania, and embarked on a four and one-half day trip across the North Atlantic all by ourselves -zigzagging all the way in an effort to avoid a German submarine attack. Without incident, we arrived on schedule at the harbor of Liverpool, England and carefully wended our way in through a fleet of vessels earlier sunk by German bombers. Much later, I found out from friends who remained with the convoy that it had taken twenty-five tedious days for them to complete the journey to England. I recall that at that point I felt once again that I had been very, very lucky.

OVERSEAS EXPERIENCES

ENGLAND

Byway of a staging base in the village of Stone, England, I was assigned to the 92nd Bomb group, 407th Squadron at a B-17 airbase located in the so-called Midlands section of the country, approximately 80 miles northwest of London. Fortunately, shortly thereafter, and because of a dearth of cryptographic messages to be encoded and decoded, I was transferred from the 407th Squadron to the 326th Squadron and assigned to Squadron Operations. Squadron Operations, with a normal complement of two officers and three enlisted personnel , and located immediately adjacent to the control tower on the flightline, had the primary responsibility of scheduling all flight crews and aircraft assigned to our squadron on bombing missions on strategic targets over the length and breadth of the European Continent. In addition it also was charged with such related activities , among others, as training new crews, scheduling test flights of damaged aircraft so as to determine their airworthiness, arranging flights to other bases for supplies and other purposes (rumors of occasional flights to Northern Ireland to procure beverages of renown for an upcoming party, or to the officer's PX outside London for any number of possible reasons, may have been factual or fictitious - - we in Operations just scheduled the flights, not the cargo). In sum and in short, any and all things relating to the flight of aircraft and crews fell within the province of the operations staff.

At first glance, it might be presumed that scheduling, including that in connection with bombing raids, would be essentially routine and mechanical in nature. That absolutely was not the case. Regularly, and generally unexpected, every conceivable type of glitch or roadblock or other untoward contingency seemed to occur. Crew members suddenly became ill or became unavailable for any number of reasons late in mission preparations and emergency substitutions in crew composition would be required (which in turn often would necessitate overcoming the inherent superstitions and suspicions of crew members for such a move). Mechanical problems in an aircraft would be discovered late in that process and neces-sitate accelerated attention and correction by whatever reasonable means were available. Sudden changes in targets by our command center, due to adverse weather developments in the original area, or for a host of other reasons, would require re-briefing of crews and possibly changes in the ordinance to be dropped. Essentially, thus, every day of a mission was an adventure because of the need to make continuous adjustments in order to insure that we pro-vided the prescribed number of aircraft available and on time for that day's mission.

The passage of several decades has dimmed my memory of many specific events and other experiences I had during the service period involved. Yet a number of recollections still remain and hopefully are worthy of being recounted. In no particular order of occurrence or significance, those which I recall and probably never shall forget include:

- The feelings I shared with others on the day of the mission, ranging from the satisfaction of a job well done when our fleet of aircraft safely were airborne and headed toward their target, to the elation we felt when late in the afternoon all planes returned safely to base, to the apprehensions first and then all too often the grief which followed when one or more of our aircraft failed to return and was probably lost.

- The occasions of joy and relief when I as a member of a team would fly down to an airbase on the shore of the England Channel to pick up the crew of a critically wounded aircraft which had managed to locate and land on the first available runway which came into view, and bring them back to our home base.

- One early morning of a day of a mission, when for some reason since lost in time, I was directed by the Operations Officer to stop our Group's planes from taking off - -necessitating a top-speed drive in a jeep directly across the grass and up the runway toward the first plane waiting to take off, and frantic arm waving intended to indicate to the pilot and to others in line who might be watching that takeoff was not to occur.

- The tragic day when on takeoff on a mission one aircraft failed to become airborne and crashed into trees at the end of the runway, the next plane in line started down the runway until it was ordered to abort takeoff and to taxi back up the runway, and the third plane which had started takeoff crashed into the latter with thirty brave young men perishing literally before our eyes

- When, on Easter Sunday 1944, on a flight to an airbase near Norwich on the Northeast coast of England, we blew a tire on takeoff for return to our home base, and our skillful pilot and co-pilot circled over our field to exhaust fuel and then brought us in safely with our wheels still tucked into their wells.

- The pleasure of spending many short leaves from duty in London - - visiting the homes of several aunts and uncles of my best buddy in the service, sharing in their family life, with regular visits to the homes of their friends and their favorite pubs.

- The day in October 1944 when I received a letter from my mother informing me that many weeks earlier my father had died, with the message having been delayed due to the difficulty my mother had in bringing herself to notifying me and the logistical problems in transporting that message overseas to me.

- The many bombing raids in London by self-propelled pilot-less aircraft (`Buzz Bombs") and longer range V-2 rockets, the devastation evident throughout that city, and the staunch will and ever-hopeful spirit consistently reflected by its citizens

- The arrival of D-Day, during which our group flew three bombing missions against enemy defenses in the invasion areas without the loss of an aircraft, and the general feeling which permeated our base that at last we had begun the final stage of destroying German military might and ultimately would be going home to our families.

- And finally, first the jubilation accompanying V-E Day, and then the following day when my Squadron Commander Officer, Col. "Moose" Hardin invited me and a group of two or three others on a B-17 flight on a long rambling journey over Continental Europe, viewing both of the ravages of war as well as the street festivals celebrating peace in seemingly every hamlet and city in every country we flew over (incidentally, it is interesting to note that Col. "Moose" Hardin later became Tom Carhart's C.O. in the Pacific region during the early days of the Cold War.)

FRANCE

Shortly after V-E Day, the 92nd Bomb Group was transferred to an airbase in Southern France for the purpose of ferrying American servicemen in a steady stream of daily flights to Casablanca on the west coast of Africa, from where they would be routed first back to the States and then reassigned to the Pacific campaign. In addition to scheduling all such flights we also scheduled leave flights on a daily basis to Rome, Paris and London. Fortunately, I was in a position of opportunity to include myself on any of such flights that I might wish, and as frequently as possible did so.

While so assigned to that location I was fortunate to be among the first group of approximately twenty or so American servicemen who were permitted to visit Switzerland. The Swiss people and their public officials, in their deft way of riding the political currents throughout history, went to extremes to make us feel welcome and to insure that we would have a memorable experience.

AT THE END

Because of the high number of service credits accumulated on the basis of overseas service and decorations awarded, I became a prime prospects for reassignment to the States and discharge following VIDay. To that end, I was first assigned in September 1945 to a Fighter Squadron located in England and scheduled to return to *this* country intact as a unit on the first available vessel. In due course, we departed from the port in Bristol England on a lengthy voyage on a Liberty Ship named after the famous patriot, Thaddeus Kosciusko, arriving in Boston Harbor in mid-October. In an emotional welcome, fireboats escorted us into the harbor and to our berth, all the while shooting tall plumes of water high into the air, and bands played loud and spirited music on the docks.

Shortly thereafter, following a brief assignment to Camp Miles Standish near Plymouth, I was discharged from the service on October 28, 1945 at Camp Edwards on Cape Cod.

Decorations and Citations: John T. Conlon

U.S.:

European, African, Middle Eastern Theater Campaign Ribbon, with six service Stars (Air Offensive Europe, Normandy, Northern France, Rhineland, Ardennes, and Central Europe)

Victory Campaign Ribbon Good Conduct Medal Presidential Unit Citation

Belgium:

Croix de Guerre, Avec Palme, and Order of Leopold 11, Avec Palme

A Squadron of B-17s assembling for a mission over Europe; note the "Triangle B" on the tail of the plane in the foreground.

Honorable Discharge

This is to certify that

JOHN T CONLON 31 261 966 Staff Sergeant

376 Fighter Squadron 361 Fighter Group

Army of the United States

is hereby Honorably Discharged from the military service of the United States of America.

This certificate is awarded as a testimonial of Honest and Faithful Service to this country.

Given at SEPARATION POINT
Camp Edwards Massachusetts

Date 28 October 1945

ROBERT L TODD
Major   CMP

John T. Conlon , Born October 27, 1923, in Worcester, Massachusetts

Army Serial Number: 31261966

Rank: Staff Sergeant, U.S. Army Air Force

ROYAUME DE BELGIQUE

Le Ministre de la Défense Nationale

a l'honneur de faire savoir   au

S/Sergeant, John, T. C O N L O N ,

que, par Arrêté de S.A.R.,le Prince Régent,du 3.1.1946, n° 1577,

il a été nommé

CHEVALIER DE L'ORDRE DE LEOPOLD II AVEC PALME,

et attribution de la CROIX DE GUERRE 1940 AVEC PALME,

"Pour leur diligent et brillant travail d'organisation et pour l'esprit courageux dont ils ont fait preuve d'une manière si remarquable par leur bravoure dans les batailles qui ont conduit à la complète libération de la Belgique d'entre les mains de l'ennemi commun. "

Il s'estime heureux de pouvoir lui adresser ses plus vives félicitations au sujet de cette nomination.

MIKE DE SHERBININ AND WORLD WAR II

My three years from 1942 to 1945 read like a geography book—of the United States. In my tour of training bases with the Army Air Corps I covered most of them. *Finally* in 1945 I completed my tour as as aerial navigator, and was commissioned a second lieutenant. Thanks to the coincidence that the casualty rate for air crews was not as great as had been feared, I was assigned to more training. I dropped cement bombs in the New Mexico desert, and became a bombardier. When VJ Day came, I was studying to bomb with a radar bombsight, which would allow our air crews to seek out targets beneath a cover of clouds. The next step was to be a B29 crew, and off to the Pacfic war.

One consquence of the war was my marriage to Polly Robinson in 1945; I had met her on the campus of Beloit College in Wisconsin,where I was in an aviation program. (Polly died in 1997; I remarried, to Jan Stevens, in 2002)

Michael de Sherbinin, 47 Triangle St., Amherst, MA; (413) 253-2037; *Mdesherb@aol.com* 8/7/03

JUDSON C. FERGUSON

Technical Sargeant
Serial #31213595
Air Force — Finance
European Theater of Operations

This is my story - 1942-1945

I was inducted into the Army on 13 November 1942, and reported to Fort Devens, Massachusetts on 28 November 1942 for indoctrination. On December 9th I departed for Fort Benjamin Harrison for basic training and Finance School. Training was completed on 15 March 1943, and I was immediately shipped out to Charleston, South Carolina, port of embarkation. I was married, and had seen my wife for only a weekend in that interim.

On 26 March 1943 I boarded with one other G.I. and a Navy gun crew, the David L. Swain, a new Liberty Ship ready to make her maiden voyage. She was loaded with military hardware and looked like a pocket battleship with twenty millimeter guns in turrets (three port and three starboard) plus a three inch gun on the bow and a 4.50 inch gun on the stern. I was assigned to the gun crew on the stern and my job was to remove shells from the shell box and hand them to the loader. We may have been a "sitting duck", but we were prepared to go down fighting.

On 27 March 1943, we set sail, hugging the coast, to Key West (March 30 — April 5), Guantanamo Bay (April 8 - 9) and Trinidad (April 17 — 23) taking advantage of the safe havens they provided. A Navy blimp also watched over us as we sailed down the coast.

Finally, on 23 April 1943 we cleared the submarine nets at Trinidad and set sail with no convoy for a destination known only to a few ship's officers. Traveling at seven knots and zigzagging periodically, after thirteen days we arrived at what we were told was the coast of Africa. We were met by a Free French Cruiser, and after they determined we were not the enemy, escorted us to the Port of Dakar, capital of Senegal on 6 May 1943.

We were greeted by an Air Force finance officer who said, "This is where you get off, men. Welcome to the 1261st Air Force Base Unit North African Division Air Transport Command."

The Finance Office was located in downtown Dakar (population about 350,000) and staffed by two officers and seven enlisted men. All enlisted personnel working in the area were billeted in six-man tents within the city limits. Our main function was to compute enlisted payrolls, officers' pay and per diem, and convert and exchange currency. We also serviced Air Force personnel stationed at emergency air fields in the Sahara Desert monthly. Malaria was rampant in Dakar, but daily doses of Atabrine were effective.

After eleven months in Dakar, I was granted a thirty day leave. I could not go home, so I chose to go to Jerusalem. I "hitchhiked" by air across Africa and back in B25's, C47's, C46's or whoever or whatever was going my way. I stayed at the YMCA, which was housing for enlisted personnel. There were only a few G.I.s there at the time.

After returning to Dakar on 5 April 1944, I was transferred to the 1269th AAF Base NADF-ATC Casablanca. I served in a finance office in Casablanca until 28 October 1944. At that time, I was selected as the ranking enlisted man with six other enlisted personnel and two officers to activate a finance office in Athens, Greece.

The finance office was opened on 10 November 1944 in the Grande Bretagne Hotel in the center of Athens. We performed our duties at that location through 3 December 1944 on which date hostilities broke out in a bloody civil war. The following is a direct quote from a Commendation issued by the Commanding Officer of the 1269th AAF African Division, Air Transport Command.

"On 3 December 1944, hostilities broke out in the city of our location. The continuation of these hostilities in the immediate vicinity for thirty consecutive days subjected every man to the deprivation of most conveniences and many necessities, and to extreme emotional strain. Many combat troops have experienced equal and worse deprivation and danger; however, it is noteworthy that the battle conditions experienced by the men of this unit were unique in the Air Transport Command and, furthermore, were undoubtedly equally severe to the conditions experienced by many combat troops. This statement is borne out in the fact that daily, for thirty consecutive days, either direct hits or near misses were scored upon the billet of the majority of the personnel by hundreds of thousands of small arms bullets, and dozens of mortar shells, hand grenades, 75mm shells and dynamite explosions. It is most regretful that, despite the neutrality of this organization, a considerably high percentage of casualties and deaths occurred, and it is sincerely hoped that our dead, along with those of other organizations, shall not have died in vain."

For this all personnel received a Battle Star and were awarded the Hellenic Republic World War II Commemorative Medal by the Greek government.

The insurrection was over in thirty days and we resumed operation. V-E Day was 8 May 1945. On 4 November 1945 I received orders to return to the States for discharge, and on 11 November 1945, I departed Athens, Greece for Naples, Italy. On 21 November 1945 I boarded the air craft carrier U.S.S. *Randolph* and on 7 December 1945 was discharged at Fort Devens, Massachusetts. Home at last to my loving and patiently waiting wife.

I shall never forget the experience I endured and considered myself fortunate to come home unscathed, and to have proudly and honorably served my country at such an historic period in time.

On my way to Jerusalem, I stopped in Cairo, Egypt,
for a little rest and relaxation March, 1944

January, 1943. "The only weekend pass
I was home for three years"

July, 1943. In front of the barraks, Dakar, North Africa

My home in Casablanca, August, 1944

DUNCAN FRASER, UNITED STATES ARMY, INFANTRYMAN, 1944, FRANCE

Duncan Fraser, Editor, author, Amherst writer, 2002

DUNC FRASER'S STORY   B 4/18/25

My army career lasted two years, four months and five days, beginning August 4, 1943, when I lifted my hand and swore to be a good soldier. I signed up for a wonderful opportunity the army was offering me, the Army Specialized Training Program. I would go to college to learn something worthwhile, which would somehow help to win the war more quickly.

But basic training came first. Mine was at the Infantry School at Fort Benning, Georgia. Toward the end of the training I was interviewed about what my college specialty would be. I thought it would be language, since I had taken three years of French in high school. But, I was told, the Army was looking for men who were already fluent in Arabic or Russian, so I didn't qualify. Therefore, I would be sent directly to "a line outfit." Or, I could opt to stay in ASTP and study basic engineering. "Yes," I said," "I want to stay in ASTP" So on New Year's Day, 1944, the would-be engineer found himself at Princeton University. We marched from dormitory to classroom, from classroom to dining cloisters, and sang, to the tune of "My Bonnie Lies Over the Ocean":

I wanted to fight for my country,
But first comes a college degree—
So take down your service flag, Mother,
Your sons in the ASTP!

In high school I had avoided serious science courses, and all math courses except algebra and geometry. At Princeton I was thrown into difficult, accelerated courses in chemistry, physics, trigonometry and solid geometry. The easy courses were English, history, geography, phys ed. and military science.

I worked hard but it didn't matter anyway—the ASTP was broken up at the end of March. I, along with 30,000 other student soldiers in the country, received a letter from Major J. A. Ulio, the adjutant general, which said, among other things, "The time has come for you to be assigned to other duty, to break the enemy's defenses, to hit them with the full weight of America's manpower."

So on April Fool's Day of 1944 I found myself in the shadow of Pike's Peak, at Camp Carson, Colorado, assigned to Major General Terry Allen's night fighting 104th Timberwolf Division. The general wanted us to "get hard, get smart, get tough," so all that spring and summer we practiced infantry tactics. In late August, 24 troop trains took the division to Camp Kilmer, New Jersey. Three troopships, part of one of the largest convoys of the war, landed us at Utah Beach, Normandy on September 7, the first division to be landed directly on the continent—all others before had gone through England.

We pitched our pup tents in the apple orchards of Normandy, and I got a chance to practice my high school French. We found that a drink of fiery Calvados would keep you warm all night. It worked pretty well in your cigarette lighter, too. From our beachhead, vital ammunition and supplies were being sent to the front by train, and also by truck on the Red Ball highway. French looters and black market thieves were stealing supplies from trucks and trains, and for a month our division was assigned the duty of guarding the rail lines and the truck routes of the Red Ball highway.

Finally, in mid-October, we rode in the famous 40-and-eight railroad cars (40 men or eight horses) to a bivouac area near Brussels, and within a few days we were pushing forward, to drive the Germans out of the port of Antwerp. By the end of October we had reached the Mark River, crossed it and were soon pinned down by fire from German rifles, mortars, artillery and a fearsome German tiger tank. In the middle of the night the Germans counter-attacked. Everybody left and ran back toward the river.

But not quite everybody. My buddy Bill Hanson and I were sleeping the sleep of the dead, and woke only to find everybody had left. We scrambled out of our shallow foxhole and ran, too, but lost our way. The sky was lighted by German flares, and we found ourselves between two haystacks. We found a shallow hole which we shared with Frank Hedden, a tall, southern lieutenant from another company, who was afflicted with the runs. We stayed in that hole for three days while bullets whizzed over us, until the rest of our regiment, after proper artillery preparation, came across the river again and we were sent back to a hospital to recover from exposure.

After that we were trucked to Germany, where we relieved the First Division at Aachen. In the weeks to come we made several night attacks and spent the winter waiting for the Roer River dams to be captured by Montgomery's slow British troops. We stayed in the town of Mercken, in an abandoned house, cleaning our weapons and playing solitaire.

My squad mate, John Fink, had bought a Belgian P-38 pistol, and was cleaning it when it accidentally went off. The slug entered the wall half an inch from where my head was—one of my several close calls.

Finally, in the early dark, cold morning of February 23, we crossed the Roer River in assault boats and thus began the final push to Berlin. We used to joke about getting an "ace," a wound that didn't hurt, didn't do any lasting damage, but was just enough to get you out of the combat zone. The rest of the outfit went on and met the Russians at the Elbe River. Not me. I was hit by mortar shrapnel the first day across the river, and luckily it was a wound in a fleshy area, specifically my right buttock. That was why they called me half fast.

Five days later I found myself in a general hospital in England, and when I was judged to be healed, I was sent back to my division in Germany. First, I was given a hospital furlough and was lucky enough to be in Glasgow, Scotland, the country of my ancestors, on VE day.

Then, with other men who had recovered from wounds, I crossed the English channel and took the 40-and-8 train to where the Timberwolf Division was, in Seeben, Germany, 100 miles southwest of Berlin. Next week the division was sent back across Germany and France again to the so-called cigarette camps near Le Havre on the French coast. We were put aboard transport ships and were taken home for 30-day furloughs. After that we were to be sent to Camp St. Luis Obispo in California for intensive amphibious training to prepare us for our assault on the mainland of Japan.

Luckily for us, during our furloughs the atomic bombs were dropped, and the Japanese surrendered. We were still sent to the west coast, but the amphibious assault training was canceled. I spent a few weeks swimming and sunning on California beaches until the Timberwolf Division was deactivated.

While waiting to acquire the requisite 45 points, I spent a couple of months as an MP at Fort Lawton, Washington, a port of debarkation for troops returning from the Aleutians. I was discharged at nearby Fort Lewis on December 9, 1945, and was home in time for Christmas.

After infantry basic at Fort Benning, GA, I was assigned to ASTP at Princeton University. Home on pass, with the lamp of knowledge patch on my left shoulder.

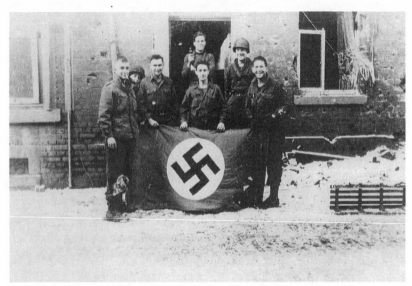

*Trophy of war—John Fink, Kelly (peeking out), Bill
Hanson, Charlie Howard, Dunc Fraser and Irving
"Jerry" Pearl with Nazi swastika flag. Lawrence "Supe"
Supernaw is at rear center; he may be holding a captured
weapon. The flag belonged to Charlie, who mailed it
home, along with a print of this picture, from Merken.*

*Posing in the upper bedroom of a house in Merken in
which the entire front wall had been bombed away.
Fraser, Howard L. Parnel (in rear), Pearl, Kelly (with
fedora) and Bob "Red" Barclay of Mayfield, Kentucky.*

AUTOBIOGRAPHY OF DUNCAN H. FRASER
ARMY DAYS 1943-1945
PART TWO—I GO OVERSEAS

The 104th Division is committed to combat in Belgium and Holland, to drive the Germans from the coast and free up the port of Antwerp. Thence to Aachen and slow progress until we had taken all the land west of the Roer River. During this river crossing I am wounded, and after weeks in English hospitals I rejoin the Timberwolves in Germany a few days after VE Day

GETTING THERE IS HALF THE FUN

On Saturday, August 26, 1944, the men of C Company, carrying their heavy duffel bags and rifles, and wearing their steel helmets, cartridge belts with canteen and first aid pouches, were taken by train from Camp Kilmer to the New Jersey shore. At one city the train stopped for a few minutes. We waved at the people on the platform, the last American civilians we were to see for a long time. Within minutes we were carrying our gear aboard a ferry to cross the Hudson River. "Where do we sleep on this boat?" asked Fink. It took the crowded ferryboat about an hour to cross to the pier where our troopship was tied up. As we waited on the pier, a Women's Army Corps band played

"Just Forty-five Minutes From Broadway." Red Cross ladies served coffee, lemonade, doughnuts and Hershey bars, and handed each of us a little kit containing needle, thread, toothbrush, toothpaste, some writing paper and envelopes, and other necessities.

A checker yelled "Fraser!" and I answered "Duncan H.!" as I had been instructed, and staggered up the steep gangplank of the US Army Transport the SS *Cristobal*, which carried the 415th regiment less the third battalion. Other units of the division were loaded aboard other troop transports: the USS *Lejeune*, the USS *George Washington* and the SS *Ocean Mail*. The men of C Company, plus half another company, were put in compartment five, three decks down, next to the bottom, I thought.

At noon on a sunny Sunday, August 27, we slipped away from the New York pier and headed out to join the other ships of our 56-ship convoy. We were later to learn it was the largest convoy ever to cross the Atlantic. Our division was the first to cross from the United States directly to France. The *Cristobal*, a moderate sized cruise ship, was built by the Panama Canal Company in 1939 to carry passengers and commercial cargo between New York and *Cristobal*, Panama. During the crossing from New York to Normandy, I wrote a condemnation of all troopships. But I must say, in the wisdom of experience and retrospect, that conditions to come were to be a lot more uncomfortable, not to mention dangerous. Ten months later, my voyage back across the ocean to the U.S. on the SS *John Ericksson* was like a taste of luxury. But in September of 1944 I had this to say:

"A troopship, like everything else in the Army, measures up to be infinitely worse than one could possibly imagine, even when one has in mind the mental picture of the old slave ships, crowded and miserable.

In my opinion, no one can describe troopship conditions adequately except an enlisted man. An officer or a war correspondent will always have, comparatively, 100% better accommodations. To say a troopship is crowded is like saying that water is wet. Ships like this one, which were luxury liners with lush staterooms before the war, are indeed different, with all the luxury stuff and staterooms ripped out, leaving big compartments and open decks closed in to make more big compartments. These are fitted with triple and quadruple layer bunks, from six to 48 in a block, nine feet high, with 18-inch wide aisles running between them. The space from one bunk to the one above it, or below it, is hardly two feet. Our bunks are pieces of canvas stitched upon rectangular frames of pipe. One bunk contains one man, his rifle, duffelbag, full field pack with horseshoe blanket roll, his cartridge belt with canteen, first aid pouch and bayonet, plus his gas mask in a carrier pouch, his steel helmet, and his nautical life jacket which he must wear or have within reach every second from the time he embarks to the time his destination is reached and he quits the ship.

"As an ironic note, it may be mentioned that in this ship's halcyon days, it sported a nifty tile swimming pool, as all luxury liners should. This pool is minus its water now, and with a few additions makes the biggest and grandest latrine (which the sailors called a head) on the whole ship.

"This latrine, with ten stools, serves about 700 men. There are some dozen salt water taps in this latrine, and two fresh water ones, giving only a trickle of fresh water. It is impossible to make soapsuds in salt water, plus impossible also to get any dirt off one's hide. You should try shaving in salt water.

"The eternal beverage of the Army, G.I. coffee, is served in bigger quantities and the most worst (note that double superlative!) quality of any that I have ever drunk before (but not since.") I sent this stuff home on Feb. 4, 1945, after having experienced combat conditions, adding this postscript: "The troopship wasn't really so bad. Just an idea of what I thought at times during the voyage."

By Tuesday, the third day out, the convoy hit some rough North Atlantic weather as the ocean got its back up. Almost everyone got deathly seasick. I joined the others in retching up my guts over the side. For days the smell of the hard boiled eggs and other shipboard fare, much of it unspeakably unpalatable because of my weak stomach, prevented me from really enjoying a meal.

The trip over did have its elements of danger. We traveled in convoy, escorted by navy destroyers and destroyer escorts, for a good reason — German submarines were lurking in the North Atlantic, and there was a good possibility of being torpedoed. "The smoking lamp is out on all weather decks," the loudspeakers, or `bitch boxes' blared as evening approached every day. We were not allowed to show any lights above deck after dark, nor were we allowed at any time to throw candy wrappers or any trash in the water, because this left a trail that submarines could follow.

But the sun shined most of the days we were on the water, and I spent most of my time talking, watching the water and flying fish, playing cards with Lou Gregory, or reading. Clarence "Fied" Fiedler joined in interminable poker games. Fied and I slept on deck most of the nights. Once or twice it rained hard, and we got soaked. At the time it seemed like hardship (especially when I once caught a glimpse of the officers' quarters, sumptuous by comparison with ours). But the voyage had its happy moments. In the evening, I enjoyed sitting on the steps leading from the gun deck to the sun deck, watching the sunset and listening to waltzes and light classical pieces being played over the ship's amplifying system.

A PX was opened, and candy was sold by the carton, not the single bar. I bought a box of Hershey bars with nuts; Fied bought a box of sour balls. On his 19th birthday he boasted that he could put 19 sour balls into his mouth and whistle Yankee Doodle. And he did it.

During the voyage we were each issued a little book with a few French phrases and some rules of conduct to observe while we were in France. We also were given a copy of a letter to members of the armed forces from President Roosevelt. "The victory you win will be a victory of all the people—common to them all," it said in part, "You bear with you the hope, the confidence, the gratitude and the prayers of your family, your fellow-citizens, and your President— Franklin D. Roosevelt."

The French language guide booklet contained some useful phrases, but some that didn't fit reality. One was "Juh voo-DAY day see-ga-RET." But we didn't ask the French for cigarettes—they didn't have any. We were the rich Americans who had cigarettes. Every youngster would ask us, "Cigarette pour Papa?" If not this, "Gum, chum?"

NORMANDY—THE APPLE ORCHARD

On the evening of Monday, September 6, land loomed in the distance off the port bow. Later we learned this was Portland Cape, England. The next morning we saw a gray blur on the horizon far in the distance off the bow, which grew larger and greener and was identified as the coast of France. The fresh green countryside looked pretty good after having seen nothing but salt water for a week and a half.

Soon our ships were gliding into the anchorage off Utah Beach, Normandy, after a crossing of eleven days. This was the first time that an infantry division had landed directly on the coast of France without having to go through the staging areas in England. The *Cristobal* dropped anchor, and soon a fleet of LCIs hovered around us. One drew up to the side of our ship. Soon, carrying all our equipment, we were disembarked down a gangplank into this smaller craft. From this LCI (landing craft, infantry) we looked out and saw that the water on this north side of the Cherbourg Peninsula was cluttered with the wrecks of ships struck by German artillery, mortars and rockets during the great D-Day battle that had occurred here two months and three weeks earlier. Some of these ships had been painted white, I guess for easier vision at night of seamen picking their way through the wreck cluttered shallows.

"Lafayette, here I am!" one of my buddies said as we stepped off the wharf onto the beach. It had been rather rainy that day and, we learned, the day before; consequently the roads were muddy. Staggering under the duffelbags, and tired from eleven days of inactivity, we trudged off the metal float pier, up to an assembly point. We left our duffel bags there, and started out, uphill, on the long march to our bivouac area. Once we took a short break, and I shrugged off my pack and gas mask and helmet, and stretched out on the soft, damp green grass. When we got up to go, I put on my pack, with one of the pack's straps scraping along my wrist as I did. It must have been this that loosened my watch—my moisture proof, shock proof, luminous dial, unbreakable crystal, Swiss watch, for when, a little while later, I looked to see what time it was, the watch was gone.

Finally, after a long, wet walk, through the little town of Ste. Mere Église, and a short ride in army trucks, and getting lost twice, we arrived at our bivouac area about two or three o'clock in the morning. In the dark, Louis Boswell and I pitched our pup tent, on soft, grassy, moderately dry, gently sloping ground, and were asleep immediately. This was our first sleep since we had left the ship. The next morning we slept late—until about 8 o'clock. We found ourselves in a pleasant apple orchard. The apples on the trees were not then quite ripe, but we ate them and enjoyed them. That day Bill Hanson moved in with us, and we used his shelterhalf for a floor. Hanse hailed from Camden, N. J. Boswell, a buck sergeant and our assistant squad leader, was from Cleveland. We found we were near the little town of Montague. The two tiny stores did a boom business in sour cider (cidre).

"I have arrived OK in France," I wrote home. "We got here on a Thursday, right after a rain. We are on a bivouac here in pup tents. In spite of the not infrequent rains, the country is quite pleasant. We are eating C and K rations. I've lost my watch, worse luck, and haven't found it yet. Please send me a cheap one—not over five bucks. Also please send some 35 mm film, black and white and color. And in spite of the excellence of our rations, any food sure would be appreciated. Love, Dune."

Our company area had been designated as H area, an apple orchard on gradually sloping land. At the higher end was the kitchen, and at the lower end was the latrine. We dug a great many slit trenches, for bowel movements, and huge circular holes, for urination. We also dug numerous sumps for garbage. "An innumerable number," Vince Quattrochi said, inspecting the blisters on his hands. On our late afternoon trip from our tent to the latrine area, we would see Sergeant Basso applying the ointment the medics had given him to cure his crabs. Sometimes the little French boys would come in and watch him, until the order came down that no French were to be allowed in the area.

DIVERSIONS

Clyde Marino, the assistant supply sergeant, bet First Sergeant Charlie Courtney that he, Courtney couldn't dig a six by six by six hole in three hours. All day Sergeant Courtney sharpened his shovels and picks. He started to dig about four o'clock, in a spot picked by Marino. There were many roots in that spot. Marino granted Courtney time out while he removed roots. Finally the bet was called off and the men finished the sump.

A projector and screen had been set up on a hillside, where we watched movies once or twice.

After pay day there was gambling. We were paid in French francs—play money—and the crap games started. Poker was a diversion, but not a high stakes game. The high stakes boys rolled `em, and either came away quickly looking for a loan, or stayed on in the hope of cleaning up. They would stay up all night, a mesmerized, chanting group huddled around a blanket, using GI flashlights for illumination. Lou Gregory told me he had won considerable money once or twice, and sent some home. The rest he lost in a day or two when the dice went against him.

One evening we listened to a radio and heard Adolf Hitler giving a speech. He screamed and ranted, and most of us, maybe all of us, didn't know what he was saying. I wondered how long it would be before we would be able to overcome the army of this madman, and go home.

ADVENTURES IN NORMANDY

It was in the tiny nearby village of Montague that we first met the French. About the middle of our trip across we had been issued a little book telling the pronunciation and meaning of common phrases in French, so we guessed, correctly, that France was where we were headed. I found I would rather talk with the little children than with the old people. The youngsters spoke more slowly, and more distinctly, and answered in a few words a question which an old man would reply to in three or four sentences.

One day Fied and I took a little walk, and conversed a little with an old woman, who gave us a glass of cider—"cidre"—which we thought was nowhere near as good as ours, being too bitter, too sour, and too old. However, I learned that the French drank more sour cider than water.

There was a creek which was a sort of a community wash center near the old woman's house. After she had talked at great length, I gathered that she was trying to tell me that either she would wash our clothes, or that we could do them in the creek, but that we would have to bring our own soap. Soap was a very scarce commodity. All we had with us was cigarettes, so we gave her some.

Then I said, "Je desire a prendre votre photographie." She was quite flattered, and posed, and after I had faked taking the shot and putting the camera down, and had thanked her, she relaxed, and I snapped her pouring out a glass of cider for Fied.

We were allowed to use cameras to an extent, but we were not permitted to photograph anything that might disclose a location, such as signs or terrain features that were characteristic of this part of France. My problem, never solved, was to find a place that could process Kodachrome.

We remained in the pleasant orchard for about three weeks, but it seemed much longer. It was our first all-out, wholehearted bivouac. We were really roughing it, we thought. There were no warm, comfortable barracks to return to, and we knew it. There were things to see around H area, where we were camped. One was a German pillbox overlooking the beach. Another was the wreckage of an American plane that had crashed a mile or so from our area. Fied and I took a walk one evening, on our own time, to see if we could locate the plane. We went in the general direction given to us by some men who always seemed to know the answer to any question you asked them. Then we stopped to ask directions of a farmer who was milking his cow. The trouble with the little book of French phrases the army had given us had one serious drawback. It didn't tell how to understand the answer when it was rapidly spoken in the Norman dialect. I wanted to ask that old farmer, "Where is the wrecked airplane?" But since I didn't know the French word for wrecked, I asked him twice, "Ou est l'avion? Ou est l'avion?" Fied gave him a cigarette and another one for his wife. The old farmer stopped milking and started to wave his arms and talk rapidly under his whiskers. His gesticulating hand seemed to point most of the time in one direction, so, after thanking him, we started off that way, and soon came across a path that led us to the plane.

It was an American transport, probably the workhorse C-47, and there were four or five GIs removing stuff as fast as they could for souvenirs. Fied managed to wrench loose some fixture of aluminum. I took nothing. We found our way back to H area just before dark.

Once Bill Hanson and I took a walk through several small villages. We saw metal telegraph poles alongside the roads. The poles were serving no purpose at the time because the wires had all been knocked off. We saw old farmhouses and barns. The barns were made of earth or clay, with tiny windows. I believe that over the course of many years or centuries this building material had settled, and eventually the walls became very wide. The houses had thatched roofs, and sometimes the barn was attached directly to the house. There was always a barnyard with ducks or hens and a foul smell.

Sometimes the children would come out and beg for chocolate or cigarettes. Once, when they took our platoon on a hike around the area, we passed a small blue eyed blonde of five or six, and Parnell dropped out of the column and gave the little girl a whole pack of chewing gum. Parnell was from Louisiana and was illiterate. We called him Swamper. He was quiet, and didn't make friends quickly, but those who knew him respected him. But he had depths in his character which could never be fathomed by northerners. He was a good combat man and a first class scout who could move through the woods at night silently. They found Parnell's body by the river the day after we crossed the Roer.

Hanse and I disagreed violently about whether a blonde should have blue eyes or brown eyes. He liked brown eyes, while I favored blue. His favorite movie star was Gloria DeHaven. Once Hanse raised a little mustache. "Wait'll Glo gets a load of my pan now," he said.

One of the longest hikes we took was to the regimental showers, where our company was sent on one occasion. I took along my clean undershorts, and a little bit of soap. The showers were six or seven miles away, and we had to pass through some town, larger than the smaller villages we had seen, to get there. The showers were a sprawling tent affair. We undressed in one tent and hoped our wallets would be safe, while we waited in a second tent for our turns in the water tent. We were allowed three minutes in which to shower-30 seconds to get wet, 30 seconds to lather up, and two minutes to rinse off. There was soap for us to use in the pockets of the canvas that surrounded the shower area, so I saved the scrap of soap I had brought with me. When we got back to the company area, we were hot and sweaty from the hike back.

On some of the roads in Normandy the Germans had put up wooden signs painted with a skull and crossbones and a legend, "Achtung ! Minen!" On these roads I always made sure to walk in the center, and was very careful about the shoulders. Vehicle mines would sometimes be ridden over again and again, until finally the least pressure would detonate them. That didn't happen frequently, as our engineers were usually thorough in their work of mine removal. We didn't enter fields where the grass had grown high, but if a cow was in the field, it was probably not mined. The French knew where most of the mined areas were but didn't go out of their way to tell us about them.

ABOUT FOOD AND DRINK

In those few weeks in H area in the apple orchard, we ate C rations for the first few days. Then we had B rations, infinitely better. The C ration consisted of two cans: a can of crackers, a powdered beverage, four cigarettes and some toilet paper, and a second can of either beef and vegetable stew, or corned beef hash, usually eaten cold. Some months later the variety of the C ration main course was expanded to include franks and beans, spaghetti and meatballs and other more palatable food. The powdered beverage might be coffee or cocoa, which meant we had to build a fire to heat the water in which we mixed the powder. Usually the powdered drink was "Lemon juice powder, synthetic," which tasted awful, only a little better than some of the water we got. It was basically ascorbic acid, which would help a wound heal more quickly. I drank my synthetic lemon juice as a duty. Most men threw theirs away. There were a few guys who really liked the stuff.

The B rations also came in cans, only larger cans, and in a greater variety. B rations were heated by the company chefs. Bread from the regimental bakery was also included, and army coffee. Dehydrated vegetables such as potatoes, spinach and turnips, and frozen meats comprised the rest of the menu. At breakfast time, B rations consisted of one or two hot cakes, and sometimes powdered eggs. Oddly enough, everyone always went back for seconds, and the KPs had very little garbage to throw away.

Later, when we were in combat and the company's field kitchen couldn't come up so close to the line, we ate K rations. I liked K rations better than C rations. They came in a box about 8 inches long by four inches wide by two inches deep, and contained a can of meat or cheese, crackers, a candy bar, cigarettes, matches, chewing gum and toilet paper.

The D ration was a chocolate bar. There is a lot of nourishment in chocolate, I guess, so a solid bar of chocolate was compact, easy to carry, didn't melt readily, and was only palatable enough to just miss being tasty. We were told they made them this way on purpose, so soldiers wouldn't eat them as candy. Some men traded their D bars to some of the mademoiselles in return for favors.

In our company area, we had a Lister bag, a watertight canvas bag that looked like a huge cow's udder, with little faucets on four sides of it, like teats. The bag was suspended from three sturdy wooden poles in the form of a tripod. This was our water supply, from which we filled our canteens and drinking cups. When we were away from a camp area, we got water where we could, purifying it with halizone tablets.

There was no PX here, no place to buy those little luxuries which the American soldier—and I especially—took for granted, such as candy bars, ice cream or milkshakes, or even sodas. We could buy local produce, such as cider, wine and cheese. Once we bought a bottle of fiery calvados, but never bought any more when we heard that some soldiers had become paralyzed and gone blind from drinking it. Later we had some local French brandy, which was excellent.

GUARDING THE RED BALL HIGHWAY

Finally a job was found for the our division—getting ammunition, food and supplies to the front quickly and guarding these lines of supply from thieves.

We were taken by army trucks to St. Lô, where hardly one building was left standing after the fierce bombing the city took during the fighting in the days right after D Day. We stayed a few nights there in a former horse barn. Bill Hanson, John Fink and I shared one stall. Some of the 104th were put on the trains going to the front, to prevent French looters from throwing material from the slow moving trains to their confederates waiting along the tracks. Our company was assigned to duty guarding the Red Ball Highway.

Supplies were sent by rail and by truck convoy. At first French looters would climb aboard the slow moving freight trains and throw supplies off to waiting confederates. This problem was solved by putting Timberwolf guards aboard the trains with orders to shoot the looters.

Other units guarded the network of roads along which moved the truck convoys—the so-called Red Ball Express. Boswell, Hanse and I were stationed at a crossroads about seven miles from St. Lô. With adhesive tape we put the initials MP on our helmet liners. Our job was to direct empty convoys coming back from the front, and to make sure they kept going. We had an easy job; each of us stood on the corner four hours a day and went through the motions of traffic cops. We also had to keep French horses and buggies and big vans off the road. It was on this job that I got to use what French I knew and learned some more. We came to know most of the people who regularly used the two roads. Occasionally they gave us walnuts, apples and sometimes cider. To supplement our meals of C rations, we bought dark bread and cheese and picked blackberries.

Rather than live in a pup tent, as we had done in Normandy, we decided to build a little shack on our crossroad corner. Boswell found some big abandoned signs and beams, and we built a shack, with one shelterhalf on the ground, one to make one side and door for the structure, and the third stretched across the top for a roof. Several small boys, about eight years old, came to visit us frequently, and once brought dry straw to put on our floor. "Sec," they explained—dry.

One rainy night I woke up, feeling very wet. Somehow, our roof was leaking. I woke Hanse up and asked him if his blankets were getting wet. "Go back to sleep," he grumbled, and went back to sleep himself. In a minute he was wide awake and was waking up Boswell. Boswell told him to go back to sleep. Just then the shelterhalf roof, which had sagged in with a tremendous pool of water in it and had been leaking, collapsed and we were all three deluged. It was 3 a.m.

Driven out into the pouring rain, we shivered and cussed and tried without success to light a fire. We stood there, drenched, until it started to get light. We had some precious gasoline that we used for a bunsen lamp, and with this combustible fuel managed to get a wood fire started. As the rain eased off, we hung our blankets up to dry on some tree branches and set about the job of repairing our roof.

The next night that it rained one of our French friends came to our small door. "Allez au ferme! Allez au ferme!" he urged. He said a lot more that I didn't understand, but Boswell, who knew the French language better than I, explained to Hanse and me that this young man, who owned the farm on which we had camped, was inviting us to his farmhouse, which was dry and less than a quarter of a mile away. Boswell told him that we didn't have permission to leave our post, but thanked him very much for his kind offer.

We finally did get permission to live in the house, with one of us at the crossroads and the other two off duty. The farmer gave us the use of the whole top floor of an empty farmhouse he owned. We grew to like this young farmer, a former soldier in the French army, who had come out in the drenching rain in the middle of the night to offer the American soldiers hospitality.

Within a week the order came for us to move out—more important work awaited us. We were to free the port of Antwerp in Belgium so the allies would have a deep water port besides Le Havre to bring men and supplies ashore.

The last night we were in Normandy we had a party at our house for our whole platoon. Lieutenant Bill Tufts, our platoon leader, brought some fudge he had made. We sprinkled our walnuts on the top of it. Some of the men brought other things for the party—bread, butter, canned beef and salmon. Our French friend had given us a bottle of excellent, very powerful cognac.

The next day we were collected in trucks, along with other elements of our company who had been guarding other parts of the Red Ball Highway, the railroad, and the pipelines. We were taken to St. Lô, where we were quartered in a former German barracks, and ate in the mess hall there. I had a reunion with my close buddy Clarence Fiedler from the weapons platoon, whom I had not seen since we had been at the crossroads a few weeks earlier, and Lou Gregory. Lou was not only in another company, but was in a different battalion. He had been riding railroad cars between Cherbourg and Paris to keep the black market thieves from stealing precious supplies headed for the front.

From St. Lô we were taken, early in October, to a bivouac area on the Carentan peninsula, where we stayed for about a week, during which we were issued ammunition, hand grenades and rifle grenades, and any clothing we needed. We performed close order drill in the mornings, and took short hikes in the afternoon. It was the rainy season on the coast of France.

One day while we were there we walked down to the beach to watch and assist the engineers remove anti tank mines which the Germans had laid. It was good to walk on the beach, even though the wind blew the sand in our eyes, and then it rained. I picked up a few seashells for Aunt Priscilla's collection.

About the third week in October, we started off on our mission in the Netherlands. Long files of men, one file on each side of the road, marched from the bivouac area about nine miles to a train depot.

As we walked, burdened with all our gear—rifle, cartridge belt with ammunition, an ammo bag of hand grenades, gas mask and steel helmet a jeep passed us, bearing the license plate "Chief Timberwolf." It was General Terry Allen. We took a break near an army hospital, and the patients in their dark red robes came out to watch us go by and talk with us. One of them told me he had been there about six weeks with an ingrown toenail. He had only got to see a few days of combat.

Finally we arrived at the railroad station, and stood around and waited a while before we boarded. While we were waiting, our kitchen crew came up in a jeep and gave us coffee and sandwiches.

THE FORTY AND EIGHTS

The train we boarded was a long one, made up of very short boxcars. I had heard about the Forty and Eights (40 men or eight horses) from veterans of the First World War, and I think these were the very same boxcars. Each car was about 30 feet long, eight feet wide and eight or ten feet high. Thirty or 35 men, with the same number of duffelbags, packs, rifles, etc., were crowded into each car.

The journey took several days . with a great number of stops. There were no windows in the boxcar, but the large doors on each side remained open, with a two by four nailed at waist height across the opening so we wouldn't fall out. Fied rode in another car, with the weapons platoon. Sometimes I rode in his car, and sometimes he rode in my first platoon car. We speculated on what would become of us, recalled old times, and proposed gigantic plans for after the war.

We ate K rations and C rations, sometimes heated over little Coleman stoves. It often happened that when two or three stoves were heating rations or coffee perched on top of them, and everyone was balancing cans and rations, that the train would give a mighty heave and upset everything. Sometimes the train would stop every five minutes. At other times it would chug along for miles without a stop. There were no latrines or toilets on the train, and we relieved ourselves when the train stopped. Not knowing when the train would start again was sometimes nerve wracking. After one long interval of non-stop but slow travel, the train did stop, and almost everyone on board jumped off, taking their entrenching tools (shovels) with them. In less than a minute, the perverse train started up again, and many of the men, "caught short," had to make the best of it as quickly as they could, and run for the train, some men just making it to the last car.

In some places on that trip north through France and Belgium, all the liberated people had turned out to wave at us, and in other places we weren't paid much attention. I think the size of the crowds varied in direct proportion to the condition of the cigarette market in that place. Most of the men had saved up quite a few smokes, and tossed them one. by one to the eager crowds. These spectators would scramble and dive for them, and cheer for more. When we passed through Paris we learned a package of cigarettes brought the equivalent of two dollars.

In Belgium, people who had had no sugar in their diet for years eagerly caught sugar packets we tossed to them. George Crozier, the company's armor artificer, made a slingshot with which he could shoot little packets of sugar a great distance from the moving train.

A VISIT TO BRUSSELS

Finally we arrived at a place in Belgium where we boarded trucks, in which we were taken to our bivouac area. We arrived in the dead of night. We were in a very thick woods, in which everyone was yelling to find his area, and those already in the area were yelling out to those trying to get located.

Hanse and I pitched our tent and went to sleep. I am glad we bothered to put the tent up, as it rained during the night. The next day we attempted to line up our tents in the light of day. This was the day we got haircuts, were issued more things we needed, and waited.

One of those days in Belgium I was on KP, which I associate with eating my fill of a delicious rice pudding that Frenchie had made. We were near a resort which, we were told, had been used as a rest area for German officers. We walked there for a rare treat, a shower.

Bill Hanson and I managed to get passes to Vilvorde, a small town not far away, where we had some ice cream, another treat. We saw

Fred Hellenberg there, whom I had known at Princeton. He had just returned from Brussels, which was off limits, but nevertheless was attracting many GIs. He urged us to go there, which we did, as train travel was free to us. The train was so crowded that we rode standing, jammed on the platform. I asked a civilian to tell when when we arrived in the city. "Ici Bruxelles!" he soon announced. The city was mostly blacked out, and we couldn't see much except the interiors of those stores which were open, all of which were bars, from Gus' bar to the Ritz. We went in one and heard an orchestra play La Paloma. In another place we heard American swing, and, as Hanse didn't like beer much, we ordered some red wine, and then some white wine, just to see what the difference was. We walked by several theaters which were showing old American films. One was "The Prince and the Pauper," with Errol Flynn and the March twins, Billy and Bobby. We thought of seeing one of these movies, but there wasn't enough time. Eventually we got back to our area in the early morning.

COMBAT

This might be a good time, in this journal, to put in a disclaimer. Although I was never a coward, I never thought of myself as a hero, either. I did my part in combat, but I never came to the situation where I had to rush a German machine gun nest, tossing grenades into it. During the war I never won any big combat medals, such as the Silver Star. Of course, all of us combat infantrymen were awarded the Combat Infantry Badge. Later I was sent the Bronze Star, as a medal given to men who were fighting, under enemy fire, and just plugged away. I did earn a Purple Heart medal when I was wounded, later on, but that was a kind of an involuntary thing.

Less than a week after we arrived at the bivouac area, we struck our tents and were loaded on trucks which took us to another area from which we could hear the British artillery firing. As we approached closer and closer, I got the feeling of being forced inexorably toward physical mutilation, and wondered how I would react when we were really close up to the enemy. The next morning, Wednesday, October 25, we started out on foot before it got light across the fields of northern Belgium toward the British 154th Infantry Brigade, which we were to relieve. "Good luck, Yanks," they said, and took off on another assignment. We examined in wonder their elaborate dugouts. "Fanciest damn foxholes I ever saw," QT remarked.

I don't think we were there more than 15 minutes before we were ordered forward. We walked across the flat fields toward the border of Holland, which was not too far distant. There was no sign of the enemy, but he was there, and he saw us first, just before dark. The Germans let us have it with machine guns, mortars and probably artillery fire. We ran, dug in and shot back. Some men were wounded, including Colonel John Elliott, our battalion commander. Toward the end of the day our own artillery and mortars got close enough to go into action.

We dug in and the next day we pushed on, shooting and ducking, and the Heinies withdrew, and we advanced some more. Germans were surrendering, and one of my jobs that day was to escort some prisoners who had surrendered to the rear. They held their hands over their heads and ducked at every shell burst. Lucky guys! They were headed for safety.

Soon we were in Holland, still pushing on. Sometimes I dug four or five holes every day as we came close to the enemy and engaged them in fire fights. Once our squad drew the detail of guarding battalion headquarters. By now Major Fred Needham, the battalion executive officer, had been made battalion commander to replace Colonel Elliott. That night we were shelled by the Jerries, and I crawled into a hole and escaped the flying shrapnel. I went into the house where battalion headquarters was set up to fill my canteen, and my buddy Hanson's too. The Dutch civilians were in one hot, stuffy room, chanting prayers together in a monotone. I went back to my hole and prayed, too. I wrote a short letter home: "Have got a little mustache now. With such infrequent shaves as I have been able to get, I just neglected the upper lip a few times, and there it was. Hanse is raising a mustache, too. Another thing: for some time now I have been inhaling cigarettes. I've smoked some cigars, too."

WE CROSS THE MARK RIVER

The next day our squad went up and joined the rest of the company. We had just got there, and were preparing to dig in and get a little sleep, when we had to take off again. We walked a long way, dug in, slept half an hour, were routed out and put on the road again. We walked again a long distance, dug in, and fell into our foxholes asleep. And for most of the time it was raining. After about three hours of sleep they woke us up, issued us rations, and once more we started off. It was the middle of the night. After another considerable march, we came up to a high dike, just as it was getting light. On the other side was the slow moving Mark River.

We crossed the river in assault boats at dawn, or a little later, almost in broad daylight. There was no artillery preparation, and there was no way to get artillery pieces and armor across the river. We hadn't even cleared the Germans our of the area south of the river, and soon we were being shot at from in front and from behind. The Jerries machine gunned the bank of the river as we climbed into the boats, and soon laid on their mortars into the area where we were crossing. We left the boats on the other side, ran across fields and jumped over water filled ditches, all the while being shot at. Some men were wounded, and some were killed. Our company commander, Captain Herschel Swann, was killed in the run from the river to the bank of a canal where we dug in.

Actually, Company C, my company, was in reserve. Companies A and B were to be the point of the attack. But the three companies were all bunched together Bullets were whizzing just over our heads. We shot back where possible. A German tiger tank rumbled up and prepared to fire its 88 mm cannon at us. One of our machine gunners in the weapons platoon aimed at the little apertures of the tank and "bottled it up" and thereby won a Silver Star for himself. The air was filled with flying steel, and I was glad to crawl back down into the cold water in a protecting ditch. Our position looked untenable but we stayed there. Soon our own artillery opened up, but unfortunately, they didn't have the range. Our own men were hit by some of the shrapnel. Our losses were heavy, and we were the reserve company. I was glad to dig a shallow hole, with Hanse, and being dog tired, in spite of the bullets and danger, we fell asleep as night came on.

The next thing I remember was waking up and seeing someone running madly by and disappear into the darkness. I suddenly realized that we two were the only ones there. Fear gripped me. I woke Hanse in a great fright, and we started out alone in the general direction of what must have been a retreat. We came upon a first lieutenant who seemed rather dazed. "Why is everyone leaving?" he wondered. He was Lieutenant Frank Hedden, we later learned, from A Company.

"Listen!" I hissed. We stopped and didn't move, and heard in the direction we had come the voices of Germans talking excitedly and all at once. We turned and fled back toward what we thought was the direction of the river. Then a flare lit up the whole area, and we dropped and froze, praying the Jerries would not spot us. Every now and then we heard the whining, dentist drill scream of a German machine gun.

We got as far as two big hay stacks about ten yards apart. Some other men from the battalion had also missed the general exodus, and were as lost as we were. They were digging in there, so we dug in also. Hanse, Lieutenant Hedden and I dug a three-man foxhole, shallow, and crawled in, wet and shivering. I don't know why we didn't continue on and try to find the river and cross back over, but we didn't. Hedden took off his shoes and socks, and hung up his socks to dry, which they didn't. He had a case of the GI trots, and every so often would have to dig a hole in the bottom of our foxhole, pull down his britches and relieve himself, then cover up the hole. I think we had a shelter half to cover us, which provided a measure of concealment and a little bit of warmth. But, in early November, it was bone chilling cold.

That night the haystack opposite us was set on fire by tracer bullets. I always thought the Jerries did it, but later I learned the order to ignite the haystacks had come from our own corps headquarters. Had it not been for the favorable direction of the wind, from the north, we would have been smoked out, targets for the Jerry machine gunners. As it was, they sniped at us and landed some mortar shells close to us, but we lay low—literally—in our hole and managed to stay alive. Fighting back, at at that point, was pretty much out of the question. In all, we were in that hole for three nights and two days. On the second day Lieutenant Hedden found part of a D ration—a soggy chocolate bar—in his pocket and shared it with Hanse and me. For water we shared what we had in our canteens. The hole wasn't by any means big enough for three, and considering the time we were in there, it was a wonder we didn't have all sorts of cramps when we did get out.

Some of the other men, from another company, dug in between the two haystacks tried to make a break for the river one afternoon. One man hesitated and was killed by a German machine gunner. It took him a long time to die. I learned later that when we crossed the Mark to make our ill fated assault, we hadn't even secured our own, or south side of the river. Thus we were being fired upon by Germans to the front and Germans behind us.

On the third night, our artillery opened up a tremendous barrage. We heard the shells whistling overhead, and the crash of tremendous explosions as they found their targets. We sweated out that barrage, hoping there would be no short rounds falling on us. But we were overjoyed because we knew the barrage heralded another attack by our battalion or another battalion. Sure enough, soon the artillery gave way to. American machine gun fire, and before long some of the attackers came up to our hole with grenades and rifles poised.

"Who's there?" one demanded.

"Couple of guys from C Company, 415th, and a lieutenant from A Company," I replied. They were as relieved as we were. They had been told to watch for the 60-odd men who were trapped north of the Mark River. In a short time a medic arrived and told us to go back with him to the other side of the river. We hobbled on stiff joints back to the Mark, and were taken across in one of the boats the attackers had come over in, and in the rain and dark worked our way back to the battalion aid station.

It's hard to describe the feeling of relief at getting out of that hole and back from the no man's land between the lines. We had thought many times we were goners, but going back to a place that was at least 90 per cent safe was like getting another chance. We went in an ambulance to the clearing station, and Hanse and Frank Hedden were taken to another hospital. I stayed for three or four days in the clearing station. I don't know why they went to the hospital and I didn't. We all had "exposure and exhaustion," marked on our tags. Maybe I looked too healthy to be sent to the hospital.

BLESSED REST

In any event I got a wonderful rest there, which I was greatly in need of. We had arrived about 3 o'clock in the morning, and the attendant gave me a cup of cocoa and a sleeping pill. I went to sleep immediately in that warm, quiet place. I woke up to find the friendly attendant presenting me with a breakfast tray. I wolfed it down and went to sleep again. It must have been late in the afternoon when I woke, and was conscious of a familiar form standing over me. It was Fied, who had been taken there because he had pulled something in his leg during the attack. I was delighted to see him, and he told me things that had happened while we lost sheep were away from the company. He said there had been a big mail call, and there were a lot of letters waiting for me back at the company area.

The "clearing station," where wounded men were either sent on to general hospitals in Europe or the U.S. (or back to battle) was located in a nunnery, and the order of nuns had lent the premises to the division's medical arm. Every day the nuns brought large sweet pears and apples for the patients. I got talking to the patient beside me and found out he had been at Fort Benning with me. I think his name as Donlon. I also had the time and opportunity to send some letters home, to tell the folks I'd had a "harrowing experience," but that I was OK. Sometimes they read about battles the Timberwolves were in before we even knew where we were or what we were doing. "Am enclosing some Belgian paper money," I wrote to my brother. "Also have some Belgian coins for your collection. The 20 francs I'm sending is pretty beat up because it went into the ditch with me."

BACK TO C COMPANY

When I got back to the company in a few days, I found almost as many new faces as there were old ones. These were replacements, and their number measured the extent of our heavy losses in Holland. "Reinforcements," the army called them, but we knew and they knew they were replacements for men who had been wounded or killed. They had come to us via many replacement depots, or "reppo-deppos," after having been through the United Kingdom.

Soon, since our mission in Holland had been completed, we took off by truck for Germany. In the meantime our division had been "pinched off" by outfits on our flanks—I guess Canadians and a unit of Poles, who proceeded to pursue the retreating Germans.

We were taken by trucks to Aachen, which on October 21 had been wrested from the Germans, the first German city to fall. Aachen was taken by the First Infantry Division, the outfit that General Terry Allen had commanded in North Africa, and that had been in on the early fighting in France. There was a joyful reunion between "Terrible Terry" and the old veterans of the First when we relieved them in Aachen. The job of the Timberwolves was to act as a holding force until we got orders to move ahead. My recollection of that ancient city is that it had suffered worse destruction from bombs than St.Lô had suffered.

The redoubtable Siegfried Line, built to protect the Fatherland, had been wrested from the retreating Jerries by units of the advancing First Army. After relieving the First Division, we were quartered in abandoned German pillboxes just north of Aachen, part of the Siegfried line fortifications ringing "der vaterland." The pillboxes were small and crowded, but quite comfortable. At night those who drew the duty occupied dug-in positions on a ridge overlooking the east. I drew guard duty the first night It was freezing cold and pitch black, until the faint dawn revealed that I had turned white. It had been snowing, and the snow covered me, and the whole countryside.

A TRAGIC ACCIDENT

We were still relatively green troops, and one of the saddest accidents to date occurred while we were in those pillboxes. Sad because it might have been prevented. We still hadn't learned all the tricks of the Germans.

The kitchen had sent marmite cans of hot food up to us. I helped carry the cans from the kitchen jeep to a place outside of the head-quarters pillbox, which was located up against the protective ridge that we were guarding. A chow line was being set up there, outside the headquarters pillbox, and Sergeant Betke asked for men to be servers in the chow line. I was going to volunteer, then for some reason I decided I would go through the line and be the first to be fed. Probably I thought that I had lugged the chow from the kitchen jeep, and somebody else could serve it. So I went through the line and took my food back to my pillbox, a hundred yards away, to eat.

To keep the headquarters pillbox warm, Sergeant Henry Betke had build a fire in the stove. "Sergeant Betke," one of the men told him, "you had better not have that fire. There is smoke coming up outside and the krauts will zero in on us." But the month was November, and it was cold. Sergeant Betke kept the fire going be-cause the pillbox had strong walls that could resist artillery and even bombs.

As I entered the pillbox where I was quartered, some 100 yards or so away, I saw and heard a mortar shell explode on the hill about 200 yards in back of the headquarters pillbox. In a few minutes there was a louder explosion and I heard a man screaming. Looking out of our pillbox, I saw it was Jim McVey squirming on his stomach. The Germans, who had zeroed in on the place previously, had spotted the smoke and had killed five men with one mortar round.

We ran to what was left of the chow line. McVey had been carried inside. Both of Sergeant Lawrence Furrow's legs had been blown off.

George Budraitis, Ernest Kronstead and Sergeant Betke were dead in a heap. I helped carry Perrin Finch inside. His leg was gone, and in his soft Tennessee accent he kept crying, "My foot's cold. Be careful of my foot. My foot's cold." The warm pillbox was filled with groans and the nauseating stench of blood and wood smoke. I went back to my pillbox as soon as I could and smoked three quick cigarettes. McVey and one other man recovered from their wounds. Furrow and Finch died in the hospital next day.

Back home, the national election was about to be held. Franklin D. Roosevelt was running for an unprecedented fourth term, and the Republicans had put up former New York Governor Thomas E. Dewey to oppose him. I bet Vince "QT" Quattrochi, one of the confirmed Democrats in my platoon, $5 Dewey would win, and lost my money. QT, a native New Yorker who was older than I was, predicted accurately that Dewey would not carry New York City. It must have been a week after the election that we learned the result.

WE CAPTURE THE CITY OF ESCHWEILER

In a few days we took a long, tedious night march to Stolberg, which had been taken by the second and third battalions and was mostly secure. From here we were to jump off, after an air preparation, with the nearby industrial city of Eschweiler as our objective. The weather was unfavorable for flying for the greater part of a week, and we waited around in a cellar all of the time.

One thing I will say about German cellars. They were built to last. There were stone foundation walls and stone arches dividing the cellars into several rooms. Most cellars were very much like caves, able to withstand almost anything except heavy bombs. After our experience back at the pillboxes, we took care to stay under cover except when it was necessary to be out and advancing. We moved mattresses from beds in the house down into the cellar and slept on them. I think it was in this house where I got several insect bites. Bedbugs, I guess.

Finally, one day, in the thin November sunshine which was suitable for the Air Force to fly over our objective to "soften it up," we jumped off. We advanced halfway to Eschweiler and dug in for the night on a slag heap. The order came down that a combat patrol should go out from our first platoon. I must explain there are two kinds of patrols — reconnaissance patrols and combat patrols. The job of a reconnaissance patrol was to sneak out to find the enemy by covert observation, or to scout out and observe the kind of terrain which lay in the path of our advance. A combat patrol found out where the enemy was in a much more direct way, simply by going forward until the enemy was found, shooting at him, and getting the hell out of there.

Two thirds of the first platoon went out on that patrol, and two-thirds got back by the skin of their teeth. Lieutenant Bill Tufts, our platoon leader, led us in the deepening twilight along the side of the slag heap and into some woods. We climbed uphill through the woods, maybe three-quarters of a mile through underbrush and trees, when I saw Lieutenant Tufts, just ahead of me, aim his grease gun (a small, gangster type submachine gun) and let go a burst. I saw a campfire, and some German solders. One of them had been hit by the burst and fell. Tufts ran back quickly, yelled "Come on!" and we followed him out of there. We were followed by bursts of machine gun bullets, but I don't think the Germans knew just where we were, and they didn't follow us. Luckily, they didn't lay any mortars in our path, and everybody got back safely. But we knew where they were, and they knew we were coming.

At about 3 a.m. the next morning, November 22, we advanced into the outskirts of Eschweiler, and kept on going right into the center of the city. Although there was some resistance and the occasional crack of snipers' bullets, we claimed and occupied the city easily. Most of the German forces had withdrawn during the night, or maybe earlier, leaving only a small delaying force. The troops we had found in the woods the night before were probably part of that force. Our platoon ended up in a substantial house on the northern outskirts of the city.

It was about at this time that Lieutenant Bill Tufts was promoted to company executive officer, as Lieutenant Jerry Hooker had moved up from exec to company commander, replacing Captain Herschell Swan, who had been killed during the Mark River crossing in Holland. Lieutenant Siobanski was sent to become the leader of the first platoon.

Eschweiler had been built on hilly ground, and at one point Lieutenant Siobanski had led us in pouring rain up a drawer, or little valley, to investigate a house that had a commanding position at the high end of the drawer. In training, we had learned that you should never go up a valley unless you held, or knew about, the high ground on either side. We neither knew nor held.

Horn, a member of my squad, thought he heard someone call him from the house on the bank at the end of the valley. He walked up to the window and saw a man with a cap with a swastika on it. Horn ducked for cover, pursued by a burst from a German "paper cutter." Luckily, Horn was not wounded. Lieutenant Sibenski had allowed himself to be separated from Clarence "Smitty" Smith, our squad leader, and somehow thought it was Smitty who was doing the shooting. He was so green he couldn't even tell a German machine gun from an American machine gun! He stood out in the open, as much as he dared, and yelled, "Smitty! Smitty! Hollywood chimes! Smitty! Don't fire! Hollywood chimes!" But our password made no impression on the German, who continued to fire his paper cutter.

Finally after returning the German's fire, we got back to the rest of our squad, and discovered three squad members were missing. But the lieutenant hadn't even counted his men, and when he did find out three were missing he didn't report this loss to the company. Later that night the three got in, miraculously, having lost only a couple of rifles. One had been shot in the foot, and the other two had helped him back. We later learned the man who had been shot in the foot had been given a Purple Heart and a discharge.

My squad stayed in a large house in one of the better sections of Eschweiler for about three weeks. A few days after we took possession of the house, the headquarters battery of the regimental artillery came and set up their heavy guns in our yard and moved into the house with us, because it was the best house around there, I guess. We infantry men slept in the cellar, from habit, and they took over the rooms upstairs.

The artillery men had very good meals. Their mess and supply sergeants slept in our downstairs rooms, and being on very good terms with them, they welcomed us to eat with them any time the C Company kitchen's offerings didn't measure up to theirs. But our company cooks provided a good Thanksgiving meal, with Sergeant Wood, our C Company supply sergeant, dishing out the turkey.

Somewhere in the upper stories of that house someone found a German Mausser, a desirable rifle. But someone who found it was smart enough not to touch it. Someone else, schooled in booby traps came in, found the all but invisible trip wire, and disconnected the booby trap. As the days passed, we were beginning to understand the advice Terry Allen had given us earlier, to "get smart"

Finally the artillery left us, to go closer to the front, and we knew we were now in the rear echelon, and would probably leave soon. Infantry was and always is, by definition and preordination, closer to the front than the artillery. We waited. Three or four different plans were ready for us to carry out, and, wonder of wonders, were explained to us. But all were canceled. The tactical situation was explained to us private soldiers and non-coms on a large map — something that had never happened in Holland.

THE ATTACK ON MERKEN

We packed our stuff together and walked to Weisweiler, about four or five miles to the east. We stayed there for a few days, then our first battalion performed an operation for which we had been trained. We made a night attack. The night I won a pass to go back to Eschweiler to see what was billed as the world premiere of "Saratoga Trunk," I knew we were to make an attack that night or early the next morning.

That afternoon I checked my rifle again, having cleaned it the previous day. I put my BAR belt in order, and laid my equipment where I could get it quickly. We had hot chow that night; we'd been eating three hot meals a day for nearly a week. I wondered when we would see our next hot meal. Platoon Sergeant Clarence "Smitty" Smith distributed ammunition and grenades to us.

I went down to our cellar, read "The Glass Key" for a while by the light of a very flickery homemade candle, then lay down on one of the dirty mattresses we used as beds to try to get a little sleep before we jumped off. It wasn't exactly what you would call a sound, restful sleep.

Sometime after midnight we were awakened. Rubbing the sleep from my eyes, I put on my clothing and equipment. I wore a clean pair of Jockey shorts, size 32, which I had received in a Christmas package, long woolen underwear, my wool OD uniform, an extra shirt and sweater, my field jacket, two pairs of socks, infantry boots, gloves and a steel helmet. I didn't wear the beanie, or wool knit cap, under the helmet because I had lost it that cold day. Of all days to lose it!

For equipment, I put on my BAR belt, since I was an assistant BAR man and ammunition carrier to Bakkun, the man who fired the Browning Automatic Rifle. The BAR belt is so heavy with clips for the BAR and my own M-1 that it was necessary to support it from the shoulders by means of a harness made from cutting down an old pack. With my inadequate hips, a harness was imperative. Hanging from the BAR belt were my shovel, first aid kit, canteen and bayonet scabbard. I had been tempted to throw the scabbard away, since the bayonet was on my rifle most of the time. Over the harness I put my gas mask, and over that two bandoleers of .30 caliber rifle ammo. I stuffed a K ration inside my jacket, and two grenades. I hung another grenade by its handle from my top buttonhole, and a fourth from the bottom of the V of my jacket collar. After hesitating a second whether I should carry it or not, I finally picked up "The Glass Key" and put it in my hip pocket. My flashlight I stuffed in my right hip pocket along with my handkerchief. I usually carried my blanket slung on my back with a cord, but decided not to take it as it wasn't absolutely necessary. Besides,I reasoned, if I got to a house, I could probably find a German blanket or comforter.

So, about 4 o'clock on the morning of Monday, December 11, Companies B and C, with A in reserve, jumped off from our line of departure toward our objective. Since well after dark, a fearful barrage by our artillery had been directed on Merken, a little town of about 100 stone and brick houses, north of Duren, nestled on the west bank of the Roer River, which runs parallel to and west of the Rhine.

Our route lay across a huge field which we discovered was serrated by German trenches as we approached our objective. In the meanwhile our artillery was to provide a "rolling barrage." This meant they would keep shells exploding ahead of us and on each side of us, to scatter the enemy ahead, and to prevent flank attacks. The stratagem worked fine except for one time when either (a) we veered too much to the right into our own exploding artillery shells, or (b) the artillerymen let their pattern veer too much to the left, where we were advancing. In the dark, we found the ground to be smooth and level. A keen December wind was blowing. We crossed German trenches, taking some prisoners, and by about 7 o'clock were fighting house to house in the town of Merken. Sometimes we moved quickly, pausing only to clear a house, and at other times we stayed for a while until all units had reached the same phase line. I ate one of my K rations, and lightened my load that much. At night we found that we were halfway through the town.

We spent a sleepless and uncomfortable night. Next day we continued our advance, and discovered we had the town to ourselves. During the night the jerries had left, except for a couple of snipers. The Germans were still firing heavy stuff from a distance. We arrived at a house where we were to live for about a month, holding, waiting to cross the Roer River.

HOPING FOR A GOOD ACE

I had my camera now, and took pictures of guys in our platoon horsing around and posing with a huge nazi flag that Charlie Howard had liberated. We always joked about, and hoped for, "a good ace"—that is, a minor wound that didn't hurt much, didn't cause serious permanent injury, just serious enough to get you out of the infantry into limited service, or maybe even get you a discharge.

Still, I told myself, from a cold blooded study of statistics in the newspaper Stars and Stripes, of all the men who intercepted enemy bullets or shrapnel, only a small percentage were killed, and of the remaining number, only a small percentage were really badly hurt. So we waited and hoped. Just one short shock, and then being carried away from the mud and cold and dirty cellars to a clean hospital bed looked pretty good. There was a story that one man would stick his foot out of a doorway that the jerries had once fired a burst of machine gun fire into, in the hope they might do it again.

We even took a trick picture there in Merken of five members of our squad lined up, with our right feet sticking out, like a chorus line, while the BAR man (the martyr) lined up all the feet through the sights of his BAR and prepared to fire. Six aces at once. Of course, he never fired; no one wanted the stigma of a SIW or self inflicted wound. We heard that one lieutenant in our regiment did that and was court martialed.

All this selfish business of getting out of the combat zone was half serious, half funny. We really hoped we wouldn't be wounded at all, and that we could advance and get the Germans on the run again, and win the war, and then go home.

In Merken we were living in houses, and we were far enough back that we were able to live on the first and second floors, and not in the damp cellars. We were getting hot meals prepared by our kitchen staff.

The only thing we did not have was a barber. DeTrempe had done some hair cutting but he had been taken to the rear with a bad case of shell shock. Meltzer and I, having found a pair of scissors, agreed to cut each other's hair. Meltzer put me in the chair first and worked assiduously with the scissors and a comb, puffing and grunting as he circled me and snipped away. Everything considered, he did a creditable job. When it was my turn to be the barber, I have to admit I butchered my friend's hair. I just didn't have the knack of it, although I tried hard enough. Meltzer looked at himself in the mirror and said he liked the result. I was glad we had only one mirror. His haircut looked all right from the front, but if he had seen the back of his head he wouldn't have been so pleased.

I have mentioned close calls or accidents that occurred during those days. One took place there in Merken. John Fink and I had been playing a simple, mindless card game called chung-o-shit, at a table near the window, until we'd had enough of it. I took a book and slouched across my bottom bunk and started to read. Fink had bought a souvenir, a Belgian P-38 pistol. Still sitting at the table, he took his new purchase and commenced to clean it. The pistol wasn't loaded, of course, but it really was. It surprised him when it fired, and surprised me, too. The bullet slammed into the wall about half an inch from my head.

One cold, dark night in December, when the snow lay four or five inches deep atop glare ice on the rutted dirt road, we were rotated back to Weisweiler for some real echelon time, and relieved in Merken by another outfit. We didn't mind the march or the cold. When we got there we heard some new songs on the radio—*Don't Fence Me* In, and *The Trolley Song* sung by Judy Garland. Back in Weisweiler, we had regular hot meals and a training schedule. They brought our duffelbags up and I got my camera, and took some pictures, developing this film and another I had taken on the line, and making prints.

It was December 16, and then, surprising to all of us, the Germans mounted a last ditch assault in an attempt to break through to the Atlantic and drive us off the continent. They made a good attempt, too. In the first part of January, when it became apparent that we would contain and push back the Bulge, our battalion, which had been in reserve during the Bulge fighting, went back up to the line, to a small town named Hoven, on the Roer a little nearer to Duren.

For about two weeks we stayed there, in a house right on the river bank, ready to make the crossing as soon as the dams farther up the Roer were captured. We knew, from the news reports in Stars and Stripes, that we held the whole west bank of the river. There were no bridges across this Rhine tributary — the Germans had blown them all up. We were only waiting to amass enough strength, and for the Roer dams to be captured. Our attack was put off several times, and each time the date was advanced we were glad. Some guys, a few lucky ones, got three-day passes to Paris. Our squad leader, Lawrence "Supe" Supemaw, went to Paris, met some ladies of the night and came back with a case of whatever it was they gave him.

We were fairly close to the river, and we could look out and see where the autobahn, or four-lane superhighway, ran. A huge bridge had once carried this turnpike over the Roer, but months ago the bridge had been destroyed by the Air Force, or maybe the Germans had blown it themselves to impede our advance. We burned no lights at night so as not to betray our positions, although from time to time German mortar shells would land close to the house in which we were living. Between us and the river we had strung barbed wire, and tied to the wire were tin pots and pans, that would bang together if the wire was disturbed.

One night we heard the pans rattle on our immediate front. I called my old friend Louis Boswell, who now was in the headquarters platoon as communications sergeant, and asked him if he could have a flare sent up by the weapons platoon over our forward observation post. He said he would relay the message to the mortar section. Five minutes passed, and we still heard the noises to our front; ten, and still no flare. We called Boswell again to see if he could expedite the flare. We feared there might be a regiment of Germans crawling up to attack us.

Soon the sky burgeoned into light, and we observed a dog running around between us and the river. No Germans. Fifteen seconds later, Boswell was on the phone to us, asking how the flare was.

"Fine," I said.

"How's that for quick service?"

"Great. How did you manage that?"

"I ran up and shot off a rifle flare," he explained.

I was lucky enough to be allowed to go back of the lines one evening to see Marlene Dietrich and hear her sing Lili Marlene and other songs. I hitched a ride back to my unit afterward, and was amazed to see the great number of trucks, tanks and artillery pieces lining the roads leading to the front. The big attack was only days away.

On the night before the attack, we were relieved from our positions for a few hours, and went back for a rehearsal of what we would be doing. We crossed a rear echelon river a couple of times, and afterward were served coffee and sugar doughnuts by the kitchen staff. Those refreshments were reminiscent of the night problems back at Camp Carson, when we would march back to camp, have a snack and go to bed in a comfortable cot in the warm barracks. But we couldn't kid ourselves. We had an idea of what the real crossing would be like. We expected the worst, having crossed one river in Holland. That same night we had an air raid by a couple of German planes. I guess the Jerries had an idea of what was coming.

CROSSING THE ROER—FRIDAY, FEBRUARY 23

During the early part of the night of Thursday, February 22, we had slept some and got all our equipment ready—rifle, ammunition, grenades, rations, etc. Some of the "old" men described to the "new" men the previous river crossing we had made in Holland. Engineers who were to be in charge of the assault boats, and who were to land with us, came to our house, and it was so crowded it was difficult to find a place to sleep. I finally finished "The Glass Key," and left it there.

Supemaw, our squad leader, had gone back to the hospital because of an ailment he had contracted while on his pass in Paris. Fink, who was assistant squad leader, was left in charge of the squad. He was pretty apprehensive, as we all were. From evening until early next morning our artillery and heavy mortars had pounded enemy positions across the Roer River. When it was completely dark we carried the assault boats down close to the river, then went back to the house. I managed to get a few winks of sleep. When it was time, in the early morning, we put our equipment on and went out and watched and listened to the tremendous barrage our artillery and machine guns were still laying down on the other side. We stood by our boats, and when the word was given, we carried them to the water. I can still see clearly in my mind those circles of men, laden with equipment, lugging their heavy boats across the field in the dim moonlight, down to the water's edge. Our squad carried two boats. We had been issued Mae West belts, or inflatable rubber belts to keep us afloat if our assault boat overturned. We clambered aboard and shoved off. I immediately pressed the button to inflate my Mae West, just in case, and found it almost strangled me around the waist. As we paddled across, we could see our artillery shells crashing ahead of us, lighting up the night with their bright flashes. I was terrified, but resolved to swallow my fear.

We reached the river, waded out on the flooded banks to the deeper water, and shoved off. The swift current nearly carried us back to our own bank of the river, but we finally arrived at the opposite side and clambered out. Kelly, the wire cutter, cut through a many-stranded barbed wire fence, and, at a trot, we ran and stumbled across a couple of fields, through some ditches that were dry and others that were filled with water.

The Jerries had opened up with mortars and machine guns, called paper cutters, but, according to the news that we read later, were too dazed to open up their artillery because of our own tremendous barrage. Their machine guns fire much more rapidly than ours, though no more effectively, and were terrifying to hear, although they were not as great a danger as exploding mortar rounds.

The enemy had other weapons and demoralizing ones, too, in the form of mines. About the third field we crossed, two of my buddies, as well as quite a few other men, stepped on "Schu" mines, including my buddy Bill Hanson. I stayed with him, giving him his wound tablets, helping him off with his equipment, and helping him work himself to a shell hole which afforded a little protection. Another man in my squad, John Fink, who had suffered a wounded foot, dragged himself over, and there we were, the two hurt, and me. I had lost sight of the other boys in my squad in the tricky moonlight.

I was scared, the most afraid I think I have ever been, what with the noises of battle, the two men, and my own mortal fear to venture into that field further. I lay there with them for maybe ten minutes in indecision, praying hard, and telling them in as cheerful a voice as I could muster that the litter bearers would soon come. An aid man did come, and did what he could. Hanse's foot had been blown off. Fink still had his foot but it was paining him quite a bit.

Just about then a column of one of the supporting units came up, but we all three cried out about the mines. Upon which they about-faced and backtracked in a single file the way they had come. I joined the end of the column. We went to the end of the field and into the ditch, which was really a creek or brook, and followed it, sloshing through the knee high water. It ran perpendicular to the direction of ahead, but after a while its direction turned, and we advanced toward the front. It was very muddy in the bottom of the brook, and progress was difficult. However, I was thankful for the protection its banks afforded, and anyway it was better than the mine field. I walked way bent over, as there was some machine gun fire overhead, although some of the short guys could stand erect and still not see over the banks. There are some disadvantages to being tall.

Was I scared? Scared shitless, as the inelegant saying went. Here, as at other times in the heat and midst of combat, I began to wonder whether I would be taken out of all this if I were to develop shell shock. DeTrempe was taken to the rear when he succumbed to shell shock. I began to think this would be a way to get out of here. I knew I was sane enough, but I almost hoped I could lose sanity and be led to the rear. Of course, this didn't happen, and we kept plodding along the stream bed toward the front.

We stopped frequently so the leader of the group could ascertain his location and communicate with other units over his radio. Several times I stumbled to my knees, and once I went headlong in. It really was a job to get to my feet, considering that I had my rifle (soaked and muddy), and had been given a spool of wire to carry, weighing about fifteen pounds. Finally we came in sight of a house, and made for it cautiously. I made sure to walk in the exact steps of the man before me, seeing that we had just emerged from the brook and were on open ground again.

I saw a group of a dozen or so German soldiers, hands clasped behind their heads, being taken out of the house. The house had already been taken—and by my own platoon! I waited there, then, while it got later and lighter and pulled myself together, and put on a pair of dry socks, which became wet because of my wet boots, naturally. Besides, I had emptied about a half a coke glass of water out of each boot.

The house—or half house, what was left of it was being used as a company headquarters, and a lot of people were in there. It was dangerous to go out, because of one damn sniper, and mortar fire. One sniper victim, shot through his thigh, managed to crawl up and they brought him in and gave him first aid. He seemed very cheerful about getting his "ace." One of the boys shared his K ration with me, I having lost mine. I also had lost some letters, two rolls of 35 mm film, the 24 sheets of printing paper, and my good can opener.

About 2 o'clock in the afternoon I rejoined my company, a little farther up. They had a good sized bunch of prisoners, including a very young German lieutenant, who spoke good English. He said he was 20 years old, but he looked younger. Our platoon guide argued with him, but it made me sick to hear his bigoted convictions and faith in Hitler. He finally admitted that "some propaganda was wrong somewhere," on either our side or his. The other Jerries looked at my muddy rifle and bayonet. "Schwimmin?" one of them asked, and made signs to inquire if I had swum the river—as indeed it looked as if I had.

Then they sent the prisoners to the rear, and we were given a new mission. In back of the group of houses, toward the front, lay an open, mined field, about 700 yards across (almost half a mile), at the far side of which ran a high railroad embankment. Two platoons, they said, had got to these tracks, and we were to go next.

There was a zigzag Jerry trench across the field, about two feet deep, and in most places filled with mud and water. We started across the field, walking near the trench and sometimes in it. When the Jerries fired machine guns at us, we walked bent over in the trench. Then they started to fire mortar rounds. We lay on our stomachs in the trench. After five or ten minutes of really sweating, and during which Jerry zeroed in superbly, Les Fowler, our platoon leader, gave the order to go back. I think the reason we didn't go forward was because there was another unit ahead of us in the trench, moving slowly or stopped. Vince Quattrochi told me years later that the Germans knew we would use the trench and had previously zeroed in on about the middle of it, and were ready for us when we got there.

When the order to retreat was given, I about faced on my belly as best as I possibly could, and started to crawl. Those rounds were getting closer. As long as they outside of the trench, we were OK. I could hear the low whistle, the sickening, tremendous snap as they detonated, and the shriek of the flying metal pieces. That, I guessed, must be artillery. Because of the zigzag layout of the trench, only two or three men would get it if a round landed in the trench.

Finally it came. I had crawled about four yards back toward our lines when it landed on the edge of the trench behind me, with a great, deafening crash and a pungent powder smell. It had been a mortar shell, the kind that doesn't whistle but goes pffft bang! At first I thought it was the concussion that had whammed me in the seat of the pants, then I realized that some shrapnel must have struck me. I looked around, saw that both of my legs were intact, wiggled my toes, and set off, still crawling, in great haste. But also in my backward glance I had seen Dyer, the man who had been ahead of me, mostly covered with dirt, and not moving. He was in the spot, and trench segment, that I had just left. The round has landed on, or very near him, killing him.

(Later Vince Quattrochi (QT) told me that the order in which our squad had gone into the trench was, first, Jim King, our squad leader; second Alan Strickland, third, Quattrochi; fourth, Fraser. Dyer, a close buddy of Strickland, was in the rear, the last man of the group. Dyer asked QT if he could change places, so he could be with his buddy Strickland. So Dyer moved into QT's place in the line

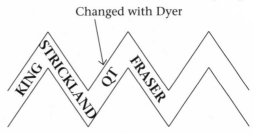

Changed with Dyer

and QT moved to the end of the squad. Otherwise QT might have been killed instead of Dyer).

We all crawled back in that trench. It was a long haul, maybe 200 or 300 yards. The Jerries tossed in one more round and let it go at that, although they shot wildly with machine guns. We struggled through deep, sticky, adhesive mud. My wound didn't hurt, just kind of prickled.

Finally the seemingly interminable crawl back through the trench ended. I looked up and saw our group of houses. We struggled out, and made a break for it, safely. The machine guns were firing at us, but not near us, and we disregarded them. They must have been a great distance away. I was mud from head to foot, literally, and heavily. My outer, waterproof pants were half off, partly because of the retarding action of the mud as I crawled, because my web waist belt had been cut by the shrapnel, as well as the belt on my OD pants. Jim King helped me out of the trench, and helped me pull my outer mud laden pants off. Then we walked speedily to the house, where I saw the rest of my squad, many of whom had been separated from the platoon as I had, and had just shown up. I had left my rifle and equipment back in the trench, and it turned out that many of the others had left their weapons, too. We'd suffered only two casualties—Dyer dead, Fraser wounded.

"Well, I hear you got your ace, kid," Jerry Pearl said. "Yes," I said, "yes, I guess I got some sort of ace." Hahn found an old mattress, and I lay on my stomach, pulled down my pants, and he put on the sulfanilamide and wrapped the bandage around me. I felt so grateful for the good job he was doing. I took my sulphadiozene wound tablets with Pearl's aid, then lay and waited. My friends came and looked at my wound. I couldn't see the wound but I could see their faces as they stopped smiling when they looked at it. They said I'd better go down into the cellar, where it was a little safer. So I did. The wound wasn't painful at all, and I thought I had been nicked, which I had, although the wound turned out to be considerably deeper than I was aware of. During the nightl lay on that old mattress, which had been laid on the family potato bin in the cellar.

During that time the platoon girded itself for battle, appropriating German weapons in place of lost American equipment.

About 3 a.m. the litter bearers came, and I and another man, who had been hit earlier the day before, were carried away, while my buddies prepared to assault the railroad tracks again. I wondered how they made out.

THE END OF COMBAT FOR ME

My four bearers carried the litter on their shoulders. I rode this way, on my stomach, to the battalion aid station, probably half a mile and about 20 minutes away.

I can recall having a great feeling of sadness at leaving my buddies while I was being carried to the rear echelon. I almost felt guilty for needing four guys to carry me. I thought I could have walked myself. I also was flooded with an overwhelming wave of relief at being out of it, with the imminent prospect of peace and quiet and safety.

At the battalion aid station, I was marked with a tag, given a cup of coffee and a one-quarter shot of morphine, although t said I really didn't need the shot. From there I was carried, on my litter, out to a "weasel," which is a caterpillar truck about the size of a jeep (or a C&R car), and on that rode back across the river, on a pontoon bridge, the pontoons being assault boats lashed side by side. The weasel left me at the "collecting" company, and from that place an ambulance took me to an evacuation hospital. There, at about 9 a.m. on Saturday, February 24, I was X-rayed and, shortly afterward, operated on.

Before the surgeon started, I asked him if he would take the shrapnel out. He said there was none to take out. Then an assistant kindly put a needle in my arm. I heard the doctor say, "About two or three CC's." I was being injected with sodium pentothol, the "truth drug."

"Now count backwards from ten," the doctor told me. I didn't even reach eight before I went to sleep, while they cleaned out the deep laceration. There were a couple of other very small scratches on my legs—the backs of my thighs—but very small, and they healed almost immediately. Later the scratch on my left thigh was to give me trouble.

I woke up hungry, for I had not eaten for over a day. I noticed they had attached a tag to me that said "Wound of buttock, moderate to severe. UK." By this I knew I was going to the United Kingdom, or England, and not to the US. Men who were wounded severely were sent to the ZI, or Zone of the Interior—the United States. They transferred me to another hospital, where I got a meal, then was taken by army ambulance to the train. I was on a litter, and the litter became the upper bunk in a railway hospital car, with bunks or litters up each side of the car, four high. My one recollection of this was my need to urinate, and my inability to do so. Finally, with the urinal or duck in my hand, I was able to pass water, and I filled the urinal and had to have it emptied, and then I filled it again.

I spent a day in traveling. I arrived in Paris on Sunday night, February 25, and was taken by army ambulance to the 62nd General Hospital just outside the city. That, I think, was the best of the hospitals. There I wrote to Aunt Helen, in hopes that my V-Mail would beat the dreaded War Department telegram that I knew would be sent to my parents. My recollection of that hospital was that it had been three or four days since I had had a bowel movement, and I was given an extra large large slug of castor oil to drink. My bed was in the corridor because the place was so crowded with American wounded. The stout French women who were the hospital aides cooed, "Choo-choo, babee. You zig-zig good, huh? Makin zig-zig my achin' back."

1945, Mar 8, AM 7:56, via Western Union — From Government = Washington DC 331A, to Mrs. Jessie Fraser, Rural Route No. 3, Salem, Conn. Regret to inform you your son Private First Class Duncan H. Fraser was slightly wounded in action twenty four February in Germany. Mail address follows direct from hospital with details. = J. A. Ulio, the Adjutant General.

Next day they took me and many other wounded from that hospital to a spacious building, a former kindergarten, I think, near Le Bourget Field. The weather was inclement, so we stayed there for the night, and maybe the next night. I slept a lot on a stretcher on the floor, being awakened every four hours to get a shot of penicillin, and spent a lot of time standing in a long line to visit the one toilet in the building. It was about then that the castor oil started to work. One rear echelon cowboy, a medic, kept asking his infantry patients if they had a German pistol that he could have or buy. I had no pistols but I kept my infantry boots near me. I knew these were also infantry equipment that soldiers behind the lines prized highly.

In the morning we were loaded into ambulances and taken out onto the field and loaded on those sturdy C-47 transport planes. I saw there was a long line of these c-47s waiting to be loaded with wounded men who were headed for hospitals in England. My litter was secured to the plane's bulkhead, and since I was lying on my stomach I got a good look out of one of the plane's few windows. We flew to a field in the midlands of England, then were taken by ambulance to a reception hospital. There were four litters in the ambulance, and my litter was in an upper position. I found myself looking over the driver's shoulder. He started off down a steep hill, and I could see a huge truck, or lorry, rushing at us down the other slope of the hill. My crazy driver kept hugging the left side of the road, and I thought we were going to crash head-on. But no, he stayed on his left, and the lorry zoomed past on our right. Then I realized that in the United Kingdom you drove on the left, not on the right. Then a short train trip to the 4173rd Hospital Plant in Malvern.

THE GENERAL HOSPITAL

This general hospital was in the country. It was something like an army camp—wood frame, one-story ward buildings lined up like barracks, with about 40 patients in each ward. We all wore blue pajamas, and had dark blue or red robes, and white canvas slippers. My slippers were too small for me. Most of my clothes had been taken away from me at various hospitals. I'm sure they were dirty and stank, but I saved my combat boots and the sleeveless sweater that Aunt Helen had knit for me. That sweater had become pretty well saturated with mud while I was in the trench. I had lost the trench knife my folks had sent to me.

Three small round coal burning stoves heated the ward. We had electric lights, running water in the latrine, and a loudspeaker which played popular and some classical music from the British Broadcasting Company. "The White Cliffs of Dover," Irving Berlin's "Dancing Cheek to Cheek" and Tchiakovsky's First Piano Concerto were popular numbers played by the BBC.

On March 10 I wrote to Fraish, "The wound is coming along in fine shape. They give me vitamin pills to make it heal faster. It used to be a little touchy, but now when they scrub it out every day it hardly bothers me." One nurse said, "My, doesn't it look nice and clean!"

Only patients whose wounds were judged to be "moderate" were in this ward. Men in my ward had small shrapnel or bullet wounds, fingers missing, etc. Broken bones cases were in another ward, trench foot and frozen feet in another, etc. Some of the men walked with crutches, some by themselves, and others stayed in bed.

At night we heard the German "buzz bombs" humming overhead. These were actually small automatically piloted aircraft, each carrying a tremendous explosive charge. When the humming stopped, it meant the little plane's engine had stopped, and the bomb would come tumbling down out of the sky. Some of these did tremendous damage when they landed on buildings, highways or railroads. But since the Germans couldn't accurately target them, most landed in the countryside and did little serious damage.

The Germans called these flying bombs "the vengeance weapon." The first of them, launched starting in June of 1943, was known as the V-1. Although Allied bombers dropped tons of bombs on the launching sites in France and Germany, they were still being manufactured in underground factories and launched at night until at least March and April of 1945. Now the V-2 bombs, not powered by an engine but real flying rockets, traveling at speeds faster than sound, were being spasmodically launched. You couldn't hear it coming. It just hit the ground and exploded.

I got acquainted with the patients in the ward and with the nurses. I wrote letters, read books and filled out a form for my Purple Heart. All my air mail stamps had lost their stickiness, because they were soaked when I had stumbled into the cold brook. A nurse found me some paste or glue to stick the stamps onto the envelopes.

Donald Van. Horn from Iowa was in the bed next to mine, recovering from some wound that, like mine, was "moderate to severe." We played checkers quite a bit. I won about half the time. He refined my poker game, playing for matches. He looked forward to returning home and starting a trucking business. He had been in the Third Army, "Patton's Killers," and had had enough war. "I wouldn't trade the experience for a million dollars," he said, "but I wouldn't do it again for two million."

Every day we read how the war was going in the Stars and Stripes. I was amazed at how fast our troops were moving. Before the Roer crossing, we had measured progress in yards a week, or maybe yards a month. Now the American armies were racing forward many miles a day, with brutal battles here and. there. But it was apparent the end was near for Hitler's Third Reich, with us pushing the nazi armies from the west and the Russians smashing eastward.

Lying there, I filled in the time by re-reading the book Country Editor by Henry Beetle Hough, and a book of essays including an essay on newspapers. I also read Kidnapped by Robert Louis Stevenson, a book of light verse edited by Franklin P. Adams, and another of good satire shorts by S. J. Perelman. I also read Don Marquis' The Old Soak, Kent Cooper's "AP, The Story of News," Muzzy's American History, James Thurber's Let your Mind Alone, Shakespeare's Hamlet, and a flock of magazines.

I was surprised to find out that one of the ward attendants there was from Bolivia. His name was Cornelio Hidalgo. He was about 30 years old. Because his English was somewhat limited, he was taking an Armed Forces Institute course in English grammar.

He had come to Newark in 1941 on a scholarship. The only English he knew was "A piece of apple pie and a cup of coffee, please." But he had set out to study the language, and then he studied airplane combustion engines. He wanted to join the Air Corps and be a flier. So he enlisted. But one has to be a citizen to be an air cadet, and he was put in the ground forces, to wait for his citizenship to be granted.

When it finally was, he had to request transfer to the Air Corps "through channels." The time delay in the official channels was so great he never was needed as a cadet. D-Day found him in a combat engineer outfit, with emphasis on the combat. He was wounded in the foot, sent back, and assigned to limited duty. He told me that he had fought in a war that Bolivia had with Paraguay, in the 1930s.

"I was only 17 years old and had to lie about my age to get in, he said. "But I carried a Springfield rifle and fought with the rest of the men."

He had enlisted against the wishes of his mother, as his father and uncle were both at the front. He said he used to cry every night. Conditions in that army were terrible. Food was badly cooked and spoiled when it got to the front. Preserved foods weren't used. Medical aid was scarce, and a badly wounded man was shot rather than cared for. There was much sickness and dysentery. He himself came down with dysentery after six months at the front. He says he thought the U.S. Army was the most fortunate army in the world— the best looked out for, best fed, clothed, shod, etc. He said that even as tough as it was at the front in Germany, this was a "luxurious war."

SURGERY AGAIN

On Monday, March 12, when my wound had healed sufficiently, a nurse gave me a dope pill, then a shot of something—I think it was morphine—and I was lugged away on a cart with wheels, along the wooden walkways between buildings, to the surgery building. There a young doctor gave me two shots of Novocain in my right buttock, near the wound, and sewed me up. I was conscious all the time. I would have liked to watch him doing the job, but couldn't, owing to my position.

Finally, the doctor said to his assistant, "There, that's one of my $5,000 jobs." To me he said, "Payday will be soon enough." He told me I would have to stay abed for probably a week while the flesh knit. He used big pieces of adhesive for a clamp, and I was wheeled back to my ward. The other patients thought they were going to have some fun watching me "come out" of ether, but since I had been given a local anesthetic, I didn't come out.

March 13, 1945, from 4173 US Hospital Plant, to Mrs. Donald A. Fraser; Salem, Connecticut— "Dear Mrs. Fraser: I am pleased to inform you that on March 13, 1945, your son, Pfc Duncan H. Fraser 31380643 was making normal improvement. Diagnosis, wound, right buttocks. Very truly yours, J. E. Pickering, Major; MAC."

On March 28 Major Pickering sent another telegram to Mother, saying the same thing.

PLAYING WITH LEAD CHECKERS

Sometime in April, I was discharged from the general hospital and was taken to a convalescent hospital, or training center located on the east-west road running between Birmingham and Coventry. Since I had arrived in early March, I had seen only the inside of the general hospital. Now a much larger and more sharply focused picture of the English countryside and the English people opened up. I saw English houses and shops, and the green English land-scape, with hedges, flowering shrubs and early flowers blossoming. I thought of the words of the poet Browning, "O to be in England, now that April's here."

Again, I had ambivalent feelings of guilt and joy. I thought of my buddies in Germany, still fighting the enemy, and wished I could be with them. I was missing so much! On the other hand, although my wound was better, the army didn't consider me ready to return to the rigors of the front. I had got too soft lying around in a hospital bed, and needed hardening up again. This was the purpose of the convalescent training center.

It wasn't a hospital by any means, yet it wasn't quite the same as regular basic training. The program lasted anywhere from one to five weeks, depending on how long it would take each convalescent patient to get back in shape. The medical people thought I would be ready to return to combat in four or five weeks. The first week was easy—gentle calisthenics, short marches through the pleasant English countryside, lectures on new weapons and tactical discoveries, plenty of free time and passes. It was, as one soldier put it, like playing with lead checkers.

The second week was more difficult. Our marches were longer, and we carried cartridge belts and rifles. The third week was quite difficult, and the fourth week found us taking a 20-mile hike with full field packs and spending a day on the rifle range. We shot with the old Springfield rifles, not semi-automatic like the Garands, but with more accurate sights. I had no trouble in scoring in the expert category with this rifle.

One day we had a big parade, with a band of trumpets and drums. Our company stood right next to the band, and the drums went oompah, oom-pah, oom-pa-pa! It didn't last long, and I enjoyed being in a parade again. I was getting back into shape, and it was time to return to duty. But first, I was to have a delay en route, or hospital furlough of six or seven days.

On April 13 the word spread around the camp that President Roosevelt had died. "Very untimely," I wrote home, "considering the world situation." I only hoped it would not harmfully affect the peace that was to come. The pace of the war, as we followed it in Stars and Stripes, was quickening. Some of the boys thought that Japan wouldn't last long when Germany was licked. I was not that much of an optimist.

One night I had a pass to Birmingham, and although nearly all the shops were closed, I had an orange milk, a glass of beer and spent about 19¢. I walked all over the center of town, saw all the public buildings, which were closed, too, heard the church chimes, and talked to a small tot by a memorial of some sort, and gave him a penny to buy a cake. They always ask, or mumble, "Any gum, chum?"—which sounded like „Er gomchom?" I hadn't seen one urchin who didn't ask for gum.

The previous September, the Timberwolf Division had landed at Utah Beach, the first outfit to bypass England on our trip to the place where we were needed. But we had heard about what things were like in England from our replacements, who were still coming to us through the replacement depots in the United Kingdom.

When I was fortunate enough to see England first hand—even though it was through the hospital chain—I found the country delightful, refreshing, and, most of all, quiet. Things and events seemed to take their course peacefully. The only girls I had became acquainted with at the general hospital were nurses—Americans, angels. At the convalescent training center, I went to Red Cross dances and met young women who were British ATS girls, American WACs and WAAFs, and maybe some civilian women. It was the first time I'd been to a dance in nearly eight months. WACS, of course, were our Women's Army Corps, and WAAFs were our Women's Army Air Force. ATS stood for Army Transport Service, and was made up of British women who drove cars, trucks and other vehicles needed in the war effort. Some of the men said ATS stood for "any time, soldier"—but I never found out about that. Dances and entertainment programs always started with the anthem, "God Save the King."

On April 6, I was paid—£16, 11 s, 2d (16 pounds, 11 shillings and tuppence), amounting to a little more than $66.25. I think by then I had a working knowledge of English money. So I went over to the Special Services office and paid for four plays I was wanted to see, and signed for two more. In all, it cost 14 shillings, about $2.80, as a shilling was worth about 20c. Thus I saw six superb, professionally produced stage plays for 70 cents each.

I was granted passes several times a week, and went to see Gilbert & Sullivan's Mikado and Yeomen of the Guard presented by the D' Oyly Carte Light Opera Company at a theater in Coventry. I saw Shakespeare's Twelfth Night, Othello, and the Merry Wives of

Windsor in the Shakespeare Memorial Theatre in Stratford. For my birthday I treated myself to Thornton Wilder's the *Skin of Our Teeth*, starring Vivian Leigh, famous for her movie rendition of Scarlett O'Hara in *Gone With the Wind*.

All these trips were sponsored by Special Services, and I loved them. The Gilbert and Sullivan operettas were performed in a Coventry theater that reminded me of Palmer auditorium at Connecticut College in New London. Shakespearean plays were presented there, too. I tried to read the plays before I saw them. I read "The Merchant of Venice," "A Midsummer Night's Dream," "The Tempest," and "Twelfth Night." I didn't see all of these.

I took an English girl to see the musical comedy at a theater in Birmingham, and bought her ice cream after the show. I took day trips arranged by the Red Cross to see Warwick Castle and the ruins of Kenilworth Castle, and had tea in a little tea room in a small village on the way.

The most thrilling experience for me was the trip on Friday, April 13, to Stratford-on-Avon, where I saw Shakespeare's birthplace. An old lady who was a docent there gave me a small silver coin, a "thruppeny bit," worth three pennies at face value, but quite rare. I watched people punting on the Avon River, and made a sketch of the scene. I saw Anne Hathaway's thatch roofed cottage, where Shakespeare courted his future wife. The old, old furniture and the household implements were remarkably well preserved, I thought. I saw where Shakespeare was buried, in the little church, as he had requested, and the inscription he wrote himself for his gravestone. And in the evening I saw a performance of "Othello."

Of the many letters I received from home, one was from Cousin Nellie Smith, of Halifax, Nova Scotia, a niece of my Great Grandfather John Fraser. She told me her son-in-law, A. Charles Light, was teaching in Hull and suggested I could visit him. Hull was a good distance from where I was stationed, but I got a 24-hour pass and made the trip—by bus to Birmingham, and train north to Leeds, then east to Hull. I arrived in the evening, called Charles, who came to pick me up and take me to his flat for tea. I had a great visit with him. He had married Marguerite Moore, Cousin Nellie's daughter. They lived in England until the war started, and since at that moment his wife and small son, Derek, and daughter, Wendy, were visiting Cousin Nellie in Halifax, it was decided that wife and children stay in Nova Scotia for the duration. Charles remained alone in England, teaching architecture. He tried to join one of the services but was told his job was essential, so he did his part as a civilian. I stayed overnight in Hull at a U.S. Army post where they gave me a bed, and I returned to my training center in the morning. I was a few hours late, but the first sergeant was lenient and didn't mind.

One day the first sergeant announced that officer candidates were being looked for. My IQ was high enough (105 needed—mine was 136), but at that point the idea of becoming a combat infantry officer didn't appeal much. I let that opportunity go by.

An American soldier whose parents had come to the U.S. from Germany, and who spoke German fluently, conducted a twice-weekly class in German. I attended a few sessions and found it fascinating. I also attended a few sessions of a class in photography.

Dad was an entertainer—a chalk talk artist and a ventriloquist—and in my letters home I reported to him about shows and entertainment acts that I saw while I was in the rehabilitation hospital. I saw a USO show with an Irish singer who sang "Rosie O'Grady" while standing on his head. One night I saw a USO show with a magician and his wife, who did a little magic too; a hoop juggler who was quite good, as was a girl singer. A Swede accordionist and a girl tap dancer were mediocre. I never did see a ventriloquist or a chalk-talk artist (Dad's two specialties) in a USO show.

SEEING THE U.K.

Finally I completed A grade, the last of my five or six weeks in the training center. I was paid and given a six-day delay en route back to active duty. My trip to Leeds and Hull had whetted my desire to see as much as I could of England, and of Scotland too, in the little time I had. During my time at the training center I had become acquainted with another private first class, Martin Godofsky, age

19, from the Bronx. He wasn't very tall and, he said, his friends called him Shorty. He told me his father had come from Russia. He had been in ASTP at Rhode Island State, and was eager to get out of the Army so he could study to become an electrical engineer. He was very intelligent, reserved, and had a great sense of humor. His Army assignment was in a signal battalion.

He knew how to play chess, and tried to teach me how. We decided to spend our furloughs together, and he agreed to my choice of an itinerary. My plan was to travel north to Glasgow, Scotland, then south to London and finally to the replacement depot near one of the ports in southern England, stopping off to spend a few days in London.

So on a sunny morning during the first week of May, 1945, carrying our travel cases containing all our clothes and possessions, we said goodbye to friends at the training center and took the bus to the Birmingham railroad station, then boarded a northbound train to Scotland. It was my first real furlough since June, 1944.

By that time the war was beginning to wind down. The allied armies were sweeping eastward over Germany and the longed-for VE-day (for victory in Europe) was just over the horizon. Passengers who boarded our train at the next station told us that latest reports were that the war would be over today. Excitement mounted as the train continued on. The latest word, as we approached Glasgow, was that the Germans had finally surrendered.

Joy to the point of delirium was shaking the city when we alighted at the Glasgow station. Through the fading daylight of that afternoon Godofsky and I made our way to the Red Cross hotel where we would be staying. Leaving our bags in our room, we joined the happy people who were singing and snake dancing through the downtown streets. We found ourselves in the square facing the city hall. The blackout was over and a string of colored lights had been strung around the second floor balcony. Soon the mayor appeared and made the official announcement — the war in Europe was over. We stayed up late that night wandering around the. city rejoicing with the crowd. Their war was over, the bombing was over, and the boys would come home. But as Shorty Godofsky and I agreed, it would be a long time until VJ day in a war theater half a world away—a world we were headed for.

In the morning we saw and heard bagpipers in the parks. Later, after phoning her, we went to visit Miss Elizabeth Wilson, a friend of Aunt Helen's, in Glasgow's Broom Hill section. She graciously gave us high tea, and we had an enjoyable visit with this charming maiden lady. She and Aunt Helen, both teachers, had met some years ago on a trip or cruise, and had remained firm friends by mail ever since. I had a few ration tickets and I gave them to her.

A few days after Godofsky and I left, Miss Wilson sat down and wrote to her friend Helen Fraser as follows:

"My dear Helen—I'm so ashamed. I meant to write immediately the boy had been, and now it is over a week since he and a friend (new) I think came. Indeed it was on V Day No. 1, the Tuesday, and I was at home about 2:30 they arrived and went about 5. We talked and had tea. I could not do much for them but console myself that they were well looked after as to jaunts and places to see. But the most important thing is that he looked well and was very bright altho still sat down rather gingerly. He's a lovely boy. Talked of school and college and everything even flowers. I liked them both immensely and it's fine to know now that the worst is really over. They may not have to go east. Let's pray they don't. He was going to Edinboro and London, and had been three times to the Shakespeare Theatre at Stratford.

"When you think of all the lovely (maybe lonely) creatures like him who have gone "west"—All round us the POWs are returning and we are getting first hand descriptions of their experiences. They certainly saw Glasgow at its liveliest — floodlighting and fireworks and the rest" That night Godofsky and I we saw Lehar's operetta, "The Merry Widow."

This first VE-day was a holiday, and because of it we got an extra day on our furloughs—time enough for us to see Edinburgh, too. I had wanted to go to Inverness, which was near the place where my great grandfather, John Fraser, had come from, but the highlands were considerably farther north, and we didn't have time for it.

So the next morning found us on the train for the short ride east to Edinburgh. Again we stayed in Red Cross lodgings, and filled our day with sightseeing. We climbed up to the castle, stopping midway to visit a camera obscura, or a darkened room in which a periscope arrangement projected a picture of the castle onto a flat horizontal surface. We wandered around the castle ramparts and looked down on Princes Street with its huge monument to Sir Walter Scott. In the park that runs along the north side of Princes Street we saw a bagpiper walking slowly back and forth, the notes of the pipes reaching us far above.

Next day we walked the Royal Mile from the castle to Holyrood Palace, and the length of Princes Street, looking into shops. I wanted to buy something with the Fraser tartan, but I had no clothing coupons, so contented myself with looking. I stopped at a photographer's studio, put on a Scots outfit—kilt, socks, booties, shirt, coat, hat and sporran, and, leaning on a ceremonial sword, had my picture taken. It was the first time I had dressed up in a "kilty suit" since I was four or five years old.

On Saturday we boarded the London train early, arriving there about noon. Two days or maybe three was all we had there. We visited 222B Baker Street, which turned out to be Madame Tussaud's Waxworks, and a few other central London sights: the Tower of London, London Bridge, Westminster Abbey, Pall Mall, 10 Downing Street, Buckingham Palace, Big Ben, and Piccadilly. We rode the two-story buses, the underground, but didn't take any taxis (too expensive, Godofsky said). We saw the movie, The Fifth Chair, with Fred Allen, and The Picture of Dorian Grey. We visited the Denham movie studios outside the city and saw the actress Celia Johnson making the movie Brief Encounter.

On Sunday, we joined a throng of Londoners walking up Whitehall toward Buckingham Palace. We soon discovered it was the route of a parade that would soon be going by from the Palace to Westminster Abbey, for a service of thanksgiving that the war was over. Soon, mounted guards clattered along the street, followed by resplendent gilt horse drawn carriages, usually reserved for coronations. One carriage contained King George, Queen Elizabeth, and

Queen Mary (the queen mother). Another carriage contained the two princesses, Elizabeth and Margaret. I thought Elizabeth was prettier than her pictures.

Sunday evening we had dinner with Mr. and Mrs. Harold Ford, a friend of Sylvia Knox Bingham (Mrs.Alfred Bingham). Before I left Salem, Sylvia had given me Mrs. Ford's address, and urged me to get in touch with her. They had both come from Stonington, Connecticut. I had phoned Mrs. Ford that morning, and she asked me to come to her home that evening, as she was giving a small dinner party. Godofsky was included in the invitation. She really seemed quite pleased to meet someone from Connecticut, as well as someone from the Bronx—as she said that she had been born in Brooklyn.

She was a gracious hostess, introducing us to all of her guests. One was Captain Nelson Pickering, a U.S. Navy officer—a captain, as I recall— from Westerly, R.I., a very entertaining man, who talked to us as equals. An English friend of Mrs. Ford explained some of the political reasons behind the war in southeastern Asia. Shorty and I returned to our Red Cross rooms feeling we had seen a little of the war from somewhat above the perspective of the foot soldier.

And thus our time in London came to an end. During that early May, it drizzled a little, but it wasn't really cold, although it had been cold a few weeks earlier. Neither were there any fogs in London. It was sunny and hot the whole time. In fact, the Saturday that we left was the hottest there, for the season, in 22 years, the London Daily Standard said.

And so Godofsky and I parted ways, he to the Signal Corps, I to the Infantry. I still didn't know whether I would be allowed to rejoin the 104th Division. I wished they would announce the outfits to be used for occupation. Captain Pickering had told us that if we were to go to the CBI (the China-Burma -India theater of war), it was not likely that my outfit would get a furlough at home.

Also, I had read in the Stars and Stripes that Military Government needed men so badly a short time ago they were accepting volunteers from combat groups. If so, I thought I would like to get into that.

A point system had recently been announced as a fair way of determining who had served and fought enough to be given discharges, and who would stay in to continue the fight against Japan. I figured that as of May 18, I had 40 points, with 45 more to go before I would be eligible for discharge. But perhaps, I reasoned, the magic number might be lowered before I had accumulated 85. Time in the army in the. U.S. was a point a month; overseas 2 points a month. My Purple Heart counted 5 and the battle of Germany counted 5. (Actually, the 104th Division ended up with three battle stars). In a little less than two more years of overseas service I would have 85. Married men with children got 12 points apiece for each child, up to 3. "So," I wrote to Dad, "if I could find a well-to-do widow with 3 children, I would be all set."

I had a little money left after my furlough, owing to a few economies we had made, such as not using cabs in London. I received a partial pay of £4, minus some to carry with me. I now had £24, ten shillings—$98 plus $4 in U.S. money.

During my travels while on furlough, I had tried to find a Dunhill pipe for my father, but I found that they were literally as scarce as hens' teeth. Neither was I able to buy any neckties for him or Fraish, or scarfs with Fraser plaid for my mother and other relatives, as clothing coupons were needed for these items.

From London I went by train to the 10th Replacement Depot in the south of England. Again I was living in a pyramidal tent, with other men headed back to their outfits. I learned two things—one good news and the other a real blow to me. I learned that I would be rejoining the Timberwolves, and not another outfit as a replacement. The bad news was that my Bulkeley classmate and friend Ray Goreham of G Company had been killed. I learned about it from a man named Herrnstein, also from G company. He said he and Ray had had a lot of fun at Camp Carson. Ray and I were at Fort Devens, Fort Benning, Princeton, and the 104th. I had been assigned to the first battalion in the 415th regiment of the 104th, he to the second.

From that "reppo-deppo" we were sent to a channel port—Plymouth or Bristol—and boarded a ship that took many troops across the channel to Le Havre. I spent a few days in Camp Lucky

Strike, one of several "cigarette camps" that served as depots for troops awaiting transport to the front. From there we were taken on the 40 and 8 railway cars, or their equivalents, through France and Germany. The country looked much different than it did when I had left in February—all the fields and woods were green, and grass covered a good part of the rubble.

By late May the Army had done away with *unit* censorship, and had only *base* censorship — which meant that I sealed my letters. The base censor only censored a certain percentage of them. Since there was no more enemy, we were free to mention place names.

By May 24, our train had arrived in Muenster, Germany, at still another replacement depot. I still didn't know where the Timberwolf Division was, but I had heard that it was somewhere in Czechoslovakia. But by this time we did know that the 104th was one of the four divisions, in addition to the First Army, which would be leaving for the Pacific sometime in June, via the States, where we were to be given a 30-day furlough.

A furlough at home! How many times I'd dreamed of that in the past nine months. It really seemed hard to believe, just as it was hard to think that the war in Europe was really over. The furlough, we'd been told would probably be from three weeks to a month. Then some jungle or amphibious training, and transfer to the fighting in the CBI or the Pacific. Well, I thought, it's better than going there directly from Europe, as was to be the fate of some divisions.

I tried to envision what a 30-day furlough would be like. Homesickness overcame me. I'd longed and dreamed so much of home and thought of so many things to do when and if I finally got there, that now I couldn't think of where to start. Perhaps I'd spend the first week in bed, and catch up on sleep. I hadn't been able to obtain a respectable milkshake all over Great Britain, so I'd make up on them, too. And pie. I'd take some pictures I'd been meaning to take. And I'd get some information from Columbia and other colleges concerning their journalism or writing curricula.

Also, I'd help Mother and Dad move to the farm they were buying if the store had been sold by that time. I'd go out on some dates, travel with Dad on his weights and measures duties around the county, and see all my old friends again. If I left on my furlough from some southern camp, perhaps I'd stop and see Bob McCall on my way home; he was at a hospital somewhere in the mid south.

I'd see some of the latest movies—with the exception of seeing the world premiere of *Saratoga Trunk*, I'd only seen old ones over here. Perhaps I'd splurge and get a good motion picture camera and projector, and miles of Kodachrome, and make some really good home movies. Or, if the folks had moved to the farm, maybe I could set up the print shop and get the paper cutter. I'd like to get a lens for the Solar enlarger and make a mural.

Or perhaps I'd buckle down and publish the "Salem Guide," just as a change of pace from my Army work. Perhaps it would be a good idea to study Chinese, or Japanese.

I was still at the replacement depot in Muenster on Saturday, May 26. After a supper of beef stew, S/Sgt. Ken Worland of Indiana and I sat eating doughnuts and drinking coffee at the Red Cross. Soon we both began to feel sick. We came up to the barracks, and there were about a dozen others sick, too. Some had the GI runs, some had vomited, and had dreadful stomach aches. I threw up—it filled my steel helmet—and went down to the dispensary, which was full of sick men. I threw up again, and the doctor gave me a hypo to relax my stomach. I went to bed, had a very wicked stomach ache, when all the muscles of my stomach contracted or hardened, and I broke into a sweat. I gradually relaxed, and went to sleep. I used the helmet once more during the night, and slept all day, missing both breakfast and the noon meal. The sickness had mostly passed by late afternoon, and I did eat supper. Almost everybody had been sick, and we guessed that the stew the night before was the cause of the mass illness. That was the second time I'd been sick overseas. The last time had been in France in October from eating too many C rations. Or it might have been the cider—or both.

The men from the 104th had been speculating how long it would take to get home. We were supposed to go in June, we read in *Stars and Stripes*, and the end of May was approaching.

"Hope I don't miss the last bus," I wrote home. "Some men are being flown home. If I should fly, I should reach the States in about 40 hours. But probably I'll go in an old pig boat. Hope we stay at an east coast camp, or leave from there on the furlough. If I have time, I'll call up beforehand; if not I'll come straight home."

I was still in Muenster on May 27, and was getting impatient to rejoin the 104th. And then we moved. Another train ride brought us on June 1 to Seeben, Germany, a small town near Halle. When I arrived back at the C Company area I had a happy reunion with old comrades. I was surprised at the changes. Many men were gone—wounded or killed, and replaced by men who had arrived after I was wounded.

In the three months that I had been away in the hospital, the division had crossed the Rhine River and, with all the other U.S. units, raced eastward across Germany, being held up periodically at places where the Germans put up resistance. Eventually the 104th, including C Company, met the Russians at the Elbe River. "They were real crazy guys," Quattrochi said.

The division had been quartered in and near Halle for the past few weeks, and was due to board forty-and-eights next week for the port of Le Havre. For me it would be a round trip from Le Havre to Seeben and back to Le Havre. From there we would take the first available ships to New York or another east coast port of debarkation. From there, men were to report to their respective induction stations, and leave from there on their 30-day furloughs. For me that would be Camp Devens in Massachusetts, the camp where I had been inducted into the Army almost two years before.

Jack Tarr gave me a whole lot of accumulated mail. There were letters from family members, from a girl back home, and from Lou Gregory and Clarence Fiedler, buddies from the 104th who were in hospitals. I also had a letter from the U.S. from John Fink. He had, he said, "a foot full of broken bones." Fink was one of two members of my squad who stepped on Schu mines on February 23 when we crossed the Roer River. The other was Bill Hanson, and he, I knew, was listed as missing. Poor Hanse. Many years later Frank Hedden, the A Company lieutenant who spent three days in a foxhole in

Holland with Hanse and me, wrote me to say he had seen Hanse's body after the Roer crossing.

Photographic supplies and a darkroom were available in the building in which we were billeted in Seeben. Since I was known to have photographic skills, I was kept pretty busy in the company darkroom, developing and, since there was no enlarger, with making contact prints. And I helped with their picture taking; adjusting the cameras they had acquired as souvenirs, determining aperture, speed, focus, etc. It was fun, getting back in practice, although I regretted that my own camera—the Argus C3—was somewhere in my duffel bag, which had not caught up with me, and wouldn't until several months later.

I did acquire a camera in Seeben. Little Pete traded it to me for six packs of butts. It was a 3¼ by 4¼, with ground glass, and an adapter for film packs. It had an f 4.5 lens, shutter speeds from 1 second to $1/400$ second, plus time and bulb exposure settings. It could be focussed as close as about 8 inches.

Otherwise duty was fairly light in Seeben. I took my turn in a four-hour shift of guard duty in front of company headquarters. One of our company officers threw a half smoked cigarette out of an upstairs window. It landed on the sidewalk a little distance ahead of me. Before I could blink a passing German had darted in and scooped up the butt, carefully extinguished it, and put it in his pocket for later enjoyment.

One day was devoted to training—mass athletics and games, and then paddling assault boats across a calm river in the warm sun. Some German civilians were rowing and paddling boats, too. It all looked quite like the Avon River at Stratford. On another day there was a battalion athletic tournament, with a party with chocolate ice cream and beer. To liven up the occasion, we heard musical selections by the regimental band. In the afternoon we went swimming again. "It is times like these," I wrote home, "that I enjoy being in the Army."

There had been time for a battalion booklet to be issued, with photos of each platoon, and the history of the First Battalion since we had landed in France nine months ago.

Wednesday, June 6, 1945, marked the first anniversary of D Day. The usual training schedule was suspended, and I went to a church service in which the chaplain blessed the men who landed on the beaches and died, and those who lived, too, so that all who came afterward could do so in comparative safety. He likened our battalion's debut into combat as *our* D Day, and hoped that we might go on in our fighting spirit, etc., in battles to come. Then Lt. Colonel Fred Needham, our battalion commander, gave an account of the outfit's actions since it landed, and stated that now, our fear having been conquered after our first fight in Holland, we would win our battles to come because of our spirit, dash, teamwork, etc.

The boys observed the day quietly, as the proclamations suggested, but I was cynic enough to think that its meaning was mostly a day of free time. When the 104th had met the Russians, the Russians, as a parting gift, had given the outfit a quantity of liquor, known as V2 juice. Nobody got roaring drunk, but a few got tipsy.

There were standing orders that American troops were not to fraternize with the Germans. I was glad I studied a little German at the Convalescent Center. It came in handy, and I was learning more at first hand all the time. One day Jerry Pearl and I, needing haircuts, went to the barber shop of a little old bald headed German. He cut our hair and used a straight razor to trim the sides and back. Another day we took a walk on a road through the fields that surrounded Seeben, up to the woods that covered a small hill. When we turned around and headed back, we met Kelly, hand in hand with a pretty little German girl, headed for the woods. A little farther on we met a woman we took to be the girl's mother, looking for her daughter, calling loudly, "Annaleise! Annaleise!" She thwarted whatever Kelly had in mind, as we soon saw the girl returning with her mother to the village.

By June 10 we were ready to leave. Next day was to be the last chance to send mail home. In preparation for the move, I sorted my stuff into three piles: Stuff to mail home, stuff to bring home, and stuff to throw away. I mailed negatives of snapshots I had sent home, and photos that my family had sent me.

On the morning of Tuesday, June 12, we packed our duffelbags, and got our packs ready, and waited for the trucks that would take us to the train station in Halle. I wrote a last letter to Dad.

FRANCE AGAIN—AND HOME

I think our route from Seeben was somewhat different from the route I had been over a few weeks previously. Anyway, I saw endless miles of railroad track, and many other sights along the way. At one station Pearl and I got off the train and walked up and down the platform. When we returned to where we had alighted, our train was gone. Another troop train full of Timberwolves was about to pull out, so we boarded it and after a few hours, at another station stop, we were able to get back to our own 40 and 8 car.

In five days we were at Camp Lucky Strike again. This camp was out on a windy, dusty plain, hot in the daytime and cold at night. We were about three or four miles from the ocean and, according to road signs, three kilometers from the small town of St. Valerie, 34 kilometers from Dieppe, 71 kilometers from Le Havre, and 71 kilometers from Lettaure. "See if you can figure out on the map where I am," I wrote to Fraish. "A kilometer, I believe, is $5/_8$ of a mile."

I spent Saturday, June 23, quite pleasantly on the beach at Dieppe, along with a number of Timberwolves, taking a short swim in the cold water (my first salt water swim in over a year) and a long sun bath, which I felt the effects of next day. The beach was a rocky one, not a bit of sand at all. And very poor in all the litter which most beaches wear—no shells, or driftwood; just a trace of seaweed and some pieces of metal and barbed wire, reminders of the famous and ill fated Dieppe raid.

That night, on very short notice, we were taken by Army trucks from Camp Lucky Strike to Camp Herbert Tareyton, located on the wooded hills above Le Havre under the trees, cool all the time with no dust. This camp was within walking distance of the harbor, so we knew the time for our embarkation must be near.

By June 24 we were told that we would be sailing on the S.S. *John Ericsson*, but we didn't know the sailing date. I figured I wouldn't be home for the Fourth of July.

Little cases of theft began to crop up. A flashlight Dad and Mother had sent me was stolen. Quite a few of the fellows had stuff taken also. It may have been a natural temptation now that nearly everyone had a pistol or more, and maybe a camera in his duffelbag, or it maybe it was because there were quite a few new men in the company.

Five days later we were still at Herbert Tareyton. "it seems like about five aeons," I wrote to Dad. "We were supposed to leave today, I believe, but the shipment was postponed for some reason or other; the Atlantic storm, perhaps."

Pearl and I found a game of "Easy Money," which is quite similar to "Monopoly," up at the Red Cross, and brought it back. So for the past few days, to pass the time, the boys in our tent and the tents around us engaged in struggles as tycoons and magnates. I read novels and wrote letters. Betty White, girl I had had some dates with back home, wrote to tell me she had become engaged to Buddy Beebe, a Salem boy who had been a year ahead of me at Bulkeley. I wrote back, wishing her well. There was also time at Camp Herbert Tareyton to visit, and I saw a lot of my old Princeton and Benning friends.

On July 2, we boarded the S.S. *John Ericsson*, and arrived in New York on July 11. The lady, the Statue of Liberty, looked grand as we entered New York harbor. We disembarked and were taken back to Camp Kilmer, where we were treated to steak and eggs, and ice cream. From there I went to Fort Devens, then by train back to New London and Salem, to start my 30-day furlough.

WAR IN THE PACIFIC AND THE BATTLE OF OKINAWA, JUNE, 1944

Amherst Rotary has two members who were combatants at the Battle of Okinawa in June of 1944. Military historians have called this conflict one of the most significant and costly battles of the Pacific campaign, since Okinawa is the closest Pacific island to the mainland of Japan itself. The costs at Okinawa were extremely high, some 5,000 killed and another 5,000 wounded in the Kamikaze attacks on U.S. carriers and destroyers. Prior to the Battle for Okinawa, the U.S.S. Franklin, a carrier, had been attacked by kamikaze planes in large numbers, and the killed were 724 and wounded another 300. The attack on the Franklin had been a test run for the more massive attack on Okinawa's defenders and the U.S. Navy vessels sent there to defend the island. Japan launched its most ferocious Kamikaze attack ever against the navy vessels deployed around Okinawa, some 240 suicide aircraft, and the damage they inflicted was severe. One Amherst Rotarian was assigned to the U.S.S. Purdy, a destroyer that was attacked and severely damaged by Japanese Kamikaze attacks. Another was a Marine, part of the invasion force itself, who lost his closest friend at Okinawa.

The accounts that follow were authored by Gerald Grady, an administrator at the University of Massachusetts, who served with the United States Marine Corps during World War II, training at Parris Island in North Carolina, traveling across the United States on troop trains to Camp Pendelton in California, and shipping out aboard a troop ship for the Pacific campaign, to an unknown destination. A close friend with whom he had trained and traveled to the beaches of Okinawa lost his life in that campaign, and it was Gerald Grady who cautioned all listening, in 1995, that "there is nothing remotely romantic about war; all war is hell." The longer account here was authored by Robert Grose, faculty member and administrator at Amherst College, who served aboard the U.S.S. Purdy during the Okinawa campaign. As this account shows, the Purdy was a destroyer assigned to the duty of "softening up" the Okinawa beaches for the invasion, and as such, it was a perfect target for the large force of Kamikaze aircraft launched by Japanese carriers against the Okinawa invasion fleet, so close then to the Japanese mainland. Grose vividly describes how the Purdy was hit by the Kamikaze attack and how the crew responded to the disaster. -ed.

GERALD GRADY'S STORY

United States Marine Corps, Pacific Theater, Okinawa

Two Amherst Rotarians were active duty United States Marines during World War II: Gerald Grady and Stanley Ziomek. Both were volunteers, as the USMC has always prided itself on the selection of "a few good men," and both were sent for boot camp, itself a special ordeal, to Parris Island, North Carolina, though not at the same time. Both survived Parris Island, and Stan Ziomek was sent across the United States on a troop train that took five days to reach Camp Pendleton in California. In the 1995 presentations to the Amherst Rotary Club, Stan recalled the heat and suffering of this trip, with crowded trains and no air conditioned cars. He remained at Camp Pendleton because the war ended shortly after he arrived.

Gerald Grady was born on November 22, 1921, and was in the United States Marine Corps Reserve in May of 1943, when we was studying at Lawrence College in Appleton, Wisconsin. He was inducted into active service that month and sent to Parris Island, North Carolina, for boot camp, which lasted ninety grueling days. He then spent another ninety days at Quantico, Virginia, preparing to become an artillery officer. Specializing in antiaircraft tactics, Grady knew his way around 50mm cannon and 90mm artillery. As an officer, he became commander of a "unit," battery. In one engagement, at Okinawa, one of his battery squad was accidentally killed by others who were firing into the air to celebrate V-J day, as their group was scheduled to make the invasion of the Japanese mainland later, had the atomic bomb been an unsuccessful strategy.

Grady's trip across the United States, some five days by troop train to Camp Pendleton, California, was complicated by his car having been "quarantined" from the rest of the train since one of the officers in his group had been diagnosed with scarlet fever. In January, 1944, Grady and his unit were "shipped out" to "destination unknown", across the Pacific on a troop ship, without a radio or regular news sources for information about the progress of the war. Many rumors spread quickly, but most of his group knew their destination: Okinawa, the nearest Japanese held island to the Japanese mainland. The principal source of information on these long trips were letters from home and unreliable rumors. However, the soldiers and marines knew instinctively where they were headed.

On Okinawa, Gerry Grady commanded a battery of antiaircraft guns, which were brought ashore in LST(Landing Ship Tanks) or LCL(Landing Craft Infantry), the type of vessel into which he crawled down the rope ladder from the troop ship that had carried the Marines across the Pacific Ocean. Once the beachhead had been secured, his Marine group moved inland, some three miles.

For personal hardware, Grady selected the M-1 carbine instead of the 45 caliber pistol. He and a good friend from Parris Island spent much of their time together, on the troop train, at Camp Pendleton, and on the troop ship that carried them to Okinawa. Theirs was the third wave of the Okinawa invasion, and Grady could not have known that his fellow Amherst Rotarian to be, Robert Grose, whose testimony is elsewhere in this volume, was assigned to the *U.S.S. Purdy,* a destroyer that was pounding the Okinawa shoreline even as Grady and his friend were leaving the troop ship to engage the enemy on the beaches of Okinawa. The two men discovered their shared experience when Amherst Rotary heard the testimonies of World War II veterans in 1995, on the fiftieth anniversary of the end of the war. Tragically, Grady's friend of training, travel, invasion and combat would die on Okinawa. In 1995, after an eloquent testimony about his personal experience, Grady turned to the gathered Rotarians and said, "All war is hell; there is nothing remotely romantic about it." And went on to say that the casualty rates for the Pacific island invasions were extremely high, and that an invasion of the Japanese mainland would have been catastrophic as casualties would have been extremely high. His Marine group had been issued fall clothing for an invasion of the Japanese Mainland, and they were understandably elated when V-J day was declared after the formal surrender in September, 1945. Four months after landing on Okinawa, Grady shipped out for Oahu in the Hawaiian Islands and then for San Diego, where his wife, Lois "Teddy" Grady, met him on the dock. *Semper Fidelis.*

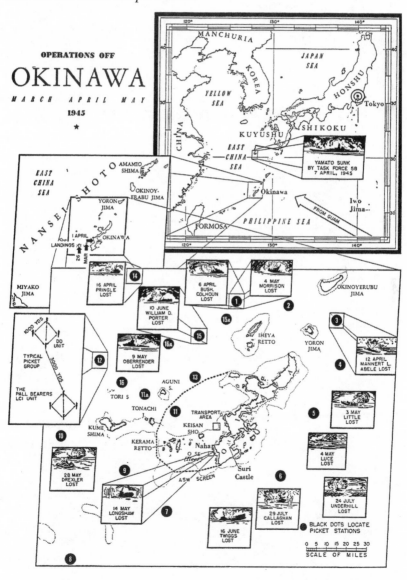

ROBERT F. GROSE

Amherst, Ma. July 1, 2003

TO ANY AND ALL SHIPS
Just now and then
when driving late
at night in rain
there comes the slap
of water in the
dark against a
shell of metal
and a whiff of
diesel brings the
midnights back, the
heavy rolling and
the funnels' sigh.

From: The Perfect Destroyer
Stanley Koehler, poet and Destroyer Officer on DD743

TWO YEARS A TIN CAN SAILOR

In September of 1941 I began my undergraduate years at Yale College and on my second day, despite my lack of knowledge of marine matters, I chose to shift from a course in freshman economics to the Naval Officers Training Corps (or NROTC). From then on, one fifth of my classes would consist of "Naval Science and Tactics".

Things certainly became more serious on December 7, 1941 with Pearl Harbor. We had physical exercises, 6:00 a.m. runs around New Haven Green, and later a training cruise to Quantanamo Bay, Cuba, on a yacht converted to a "Gunship". (We did drop some depth charges on a possible sub.)

To allow us to complete our degrees we were enrolled in an added semester in each of the next two summers. Moreover, the Navy and Yale compromised and decided that with the expanding war we trainees needed only seven semesters to qualify for a Bachelor's degree. Therefore, I found myself in February of 1944 with a) the promise that I would receive a B.A. degree by mail in June (I did); b) a rank of Ensign in the Naval Reserve, plus c) orders to report to Destroyer School at Philadelphia, Pennsylvania and Norfolk, Virginia. There we had more classes, learned damage control and fighting gasoline fires with fog nozzles in a concrete mock up of an aircraft carrier, gunnery, signals, ship handling and much more.

On July 18, 1944, 22 officers and a crew of 333 enlisted men and some of their families gathered at the Boston Navy Yard for the commissioning of the U.S.S. *Purdy*, DD 734. The *Purdy's* keel had been laid down at the Bath Iron Works, Maine, on Dec. 22, 1943 and she was launched there on May 7, 1944. The ship was named for Lt. Commander Frederick W. Purdy who was killed in action, July 5, 1943 as Executive Officer of the USS *Strong* when it was torpedoed off New Georgia Island when Purdy continued to search for a wounded enlisted man in the burning forecastle.

The USS *Purdy* was one of the 53 ship Allen M. Sumner class. Its dimensions were: Length: 376 ½ ft. Beam: 41 ft. Draft: 19 ft., Standard displacement: 2200 tons, full displacement: 3000 tons, Armament: 3 twin five inch turrets, four 40 mm antiaircraft guns, (2 quad and

2 twin bofors), 11 20mm anti-aircraft guns, 10 torpedo tubes, 2 depth charge K guns and 4 depth charge racks (anti-submarine) The ship's top speed was 34 knots.

After some repair work to align the ship's struts in the Boston Navy Yard, the *Purdy* departed on 30 August, 1944 for its shakedown cruise to Bermuda under the command of Frank L. Johnson. (Johnson had experienced heavy bombardment while on his prior command and he insisted we train and train. He used up our full allotment of practice ammunition within the first third of our shakedown. (We ordered more.) After being underway for only several days, the Commanding Officer growled: "Grose, take the conn". Needless to say, my heart stopped for several moments as this very green 20 year old ensign took over the tasks of directing the path of a "2200 ton" destroyer with its 350 passengers. (I guess I passed muster, since I was asked to become a regular "Officer of the Deck underway" in the watch rotation. My other duties included assistant damage control officer, boat officer, division officer for one half of the deck force seamen (some 40-50 men) plus occasionally typing the coded messages which came in by radio. At general quarters (or battle stations) I directed the after port Quad 40mm Bofors antiaircraft gun from a metal "tub" above the guns and the ten man loading crew.

Another new adventure awaited me when we fired practice torpedoes. Instead of TNT, these had water in their forward compartments plus compressed air that blew out the water at the end of each run so that they could be used over. Out in the middle of the wide, wide Atlantic my VERY young Coxswain and I were lowered from the davits in the small boat to chase and capture the spent torpedoes. We were enjoined to avoid getting directly over the nose of the bobbing torpedo since it might lunge up to smash the bottom of our 26 foot wooden motor whale boat. Fortunately, we snagged each torpedo and returned each time to the *Purdy* safely. Then anti-aircraft practice brought us near Bermuda, shooting at drones towed by a plane.

As we headed back to Boston on 1 October 1944, word came of a serious hurricane—soon we had to slow and the clinometer on the bridge showed a 47 degree roll both to port and to starboard. I myself saw it clearly at 52 degrees on one roll! Two old destroyers capsized and sank. We had some damage from the waves and two days later the first landfall we saw was the welcome sight of the Pilgrim Monument at Provincetown on Cape Cod.

After repairing storm damage we reported to the Destroyer Training Command at N.O.B., Norfolk, Virginia. There in October we became a training ship for new nucleus crews preparing to staff new Allen Sumner Class destroyers. We took the crews out each morning so they could practice with our ship to familiarize themselves with the key details of their future ships. We also spent some time testing five inch shells with the new proximity fuses which would explode the shell *close* to an enemy plane without having to hit the plane itself. We also had radar installed on our 40 mm anti-aircraft guns to increase our accuracy. (We were the 2"" naval ship to be so equipped.) We next sailed up to Casco Bay, Maine, for testing our equipment. We moved next on to Chesapeake Bay to aid in screening two cruisers on their shakedown trips to Trinidad.

Alone we next went through the Panama Canal, had a brief stop at San Diego and departed to Pearl Harbor arriving on 2 March, 1945. Passing next to Eniwetok, we steamed within a view of Ulithi and arrived at Leyte in the Philippines on 17 March 1945. The next 10 days we prepared for our participation in Operation Plan: "Love 1045", the invasion of Okinawa, by provisioning the *Purdy* with food and ammunition.

The convoy was made up of 26 transports, arranged in six columns, two of five each and four of four each, arranged with the longer columns on the outside. The nine anti-submarine ships including the *Purdy*, led in a semi-circular arc. Special ships and Navy "seals" had already gone ahead to secure the small cluster of volcanic islands named Kerama Retto. Later, these islands would form a refuge and harbor for damaged ships, for repairs and for protection from Kamikazes.

Landings on the main island of Okinawa began promptly at 0600 April 1, 1945—Easter Sunday. *Purdy* began its assigned 8 mile long figure eight on an anti-submarine patrol. The "old" battleships sent salvo after salvo of 14 and 16 inch shells to clear the landing beaches. On 5 April while we were continuing our days of figure 8's, suddenly shells *from* the island began to smash into the *Nevada* just 1500 yards ahead of us. (Apparently we were too small a target for the Japanese to attack.) Although damaged the old battleship soon silenced the shore guns. At first the Japanese did not contest our landing but became very stubborn as our troops moved north.

News came to us that night that the huge Japanese Battleship *Yamato* with 18 inch guns plus cruisers and destroyers was moving south, headed toward the north end of Okinawa. This was a real threat to the troops on Okinawa as well as to the radar picket destroyers. These radar equipped ships were arranged in an arc about 40 miles north of the island of Okinawa in order to repulse the waves of suicide bombers flying one way trips to bomb the ships at Okinawa. Fortunately, the air power of the American aircraft carriers soon prevailed. Some 375 U.S. dive bombers and torpedo planes sank the massive *Yamato* plus three Japanese cruisers and four destroyers.

On the 6th of April a Japanese suicide plane flew close to us but chose to try to hit one of our cruisers. We were next directed to the east of Okinawa where the US Destroyer *Mullany* (DD528) had been badly hit. When we reached her, dead men were draped over the lifelines, fires were burning in the after 5 inch gun mount, and earlier the Captain and crew had had to abandon ship. The *Purdy* eased into the starboard quarter of the *Mullany* with our port amidships. Our Captain was purported to have said to our Chief Engineer that if he "heard an explosion not to wait but to back down full speed immediately." (Capt. Johnson apparently expected an explosion there was none and he earned the Navy Cross.) Lieut. Lewis Helphand and his small damage control party boarded *Mullany* and in several hours put out the fires, so that the *Mullany's* captain and many crew were able to re-board. We escorted the limping ship back to a sheltered area to offload her dead and wounded

As various ships came and left Kerama Retto, their crews could not help but see the growing numbers of badly mangled ships. Since most of the damaged destroyers had been out on radar picket stations, we began to feel more and more anxious about an assignment to one of the picket locations. Commodore Moosebrugger in charge of the picket line wisely began to staff the radar picket stations with *two* destroyers so that one of them could serve as the control of our combat planes from our carriers, while the other DD served as support fire against the suicide planes. (Four small landing craft were usually added for support and rescue.)

On 10 April *Purdy* was assigned as fire support for the DD *Cassin Young*. Both of us were sent to the central northern radar picket station, i.e. No. 1. Fleet headquarters warned all ships to expect heavy Japanese attacks on April 12th. At 1300 on that date our radars picked up the images of perhaps 30 Japanese planes approaching from the north.

Below is what our navigator Ira W. Folden, Lt.jg, described in his fine history of the early years of the *Purdy*: (Lieutenant Folden had a good vantage point on the ship's bridge.)---

"The first planes were sighted about 1330. Some of the LCI's, LSM's, and other small craft were hit and on fire and at about 1400 the Cassin Young *was struck on the mast by a Kamikaze and their radar was destroyed.* Cassin Young *retired and there was no immediate connection between* Purdy *and the three plane combat air patrol (Corsairs) in the area when* Cassin Young *withdrew."*

"There was a constant battle between the Kamikazes and three Corsairs who were trying to intercept any Jap planes attacking our station for the next hour. *Purdy* had left Leyte with 600 rounds of 5" shells armed with proximity fuses which were soon exhausted; therefore we had to return to setting fuses in the hoist. Our Corsairs followed the Jap planes inside the 12,000 yard zone where the ships had to open up for self preservation. At about 1500 hours one of the Corsairs went down, the pilot came up on a yellow life raft and we slowed from 30 knots to just 5 knots about 600 yards from the downed flyer when we were attacked by two Japanese planes about three miles away. The two remaining Corsairs were circling the downed flyer. Ensign Edmonson, our Fighter Director Officer in CIC, (Combat Information Center) said "Chickens orbiting over downed flyer, we cannot pick up your buddy as we are under attack." Reply came back, "Roger, where are the blankety blanks?" We made a left turn and went from 5 to 27 knots in 2 minutes. We shot both of these planes down but the second hit the water and ricocheted into the starboard side of the ship about 90 feet from the bow. The plane's motor smashed a hole about three feet down from the main deck and parts of the plane fell on deck and in the water. However a 12" shell carried beneath the plane's fuselage punched a hole about 6 feet below deck level and this missile proceeded through IC (Internal Communications) room into the food serving room where it exploded, blowing out the port side, blowing up the port deck, and lifting the port 20mm deck up at a 45 degree angle dumping 3 men in the water. Maximum property damage and personnel casualties occurred in the IC room. All fire control equipment which controlled use and effectiveness of our main battery was destroyed. Damage to the port side made it impossible to fire either of the forward 5" twin mounts. That meant we had only one usable 5" twin battery operating only in manual control, however all the automatic weapons were intact and usable. At about 1630 we began our retirement to Hagushi arriving about midnight and transferred our wounded to a hospital ship.

It had been a difficult time for the after port quad 40mm gun. When we fired to port we had the feeling we had some effective short bursts. Later when we tried to fire at the lone last plane coming in on our starboard bow, we could not swing the guns far enough forward to fire safely across our own ship. When the suicide plane hit, the explosion was directly ahead of us on the port side and the smoke and fire bellowed suddenly down on our gun, its crew and into our control location. Some men jumped or were blown into the water.

We lost several of my gun crew. Overall the *Purdy* had 15 killed (including one officer) and 29 enlisted men were seriously injured plus 27 who were injured but not seriously. There were many other heroes. I was especially impressed by the black steward's mates on the 20mm anti-aircraft guns. Some of their locations were extremely close to the blasts of the five inch guns. The men did not desert their posts, even though a number of them permanently lost much of their hearing.

The *Cassin Young* had one man killed and 59 wounded on 12 April 1945, but it was back on the picket line in a month. This distinguished ship was hit by another Kamikaze plane again, with 22 men killed and 45 wounded only 16 days before Japan surrendered. At present she is a museum ship you can see at the Boston Navy Yard. It was only later that night of battle (or the next morning) that we learned that Franklin D. Roosevelt had also died on April 12, 1945. This only added to our sadness over our losses on that date.

Again Navigator Folden:

"The 13th was spent at anchor while some experts reviewed the damage and decided we should go into Kerama Retto for temporary repairs where we proceeded on the 14th and moored alongside an Auxiliary Repair Lighter (ARL) which was a machine shop in a Landing Ship Tank (LST) frame. The men on the ARL had been in the Pacific area for three years and they estimated that it would take four weeks (28 days) to make the Purdy *seaworthy."*

We had seen many horrible sights, we had taken our shipmates to first aid stations, to hospitals and to the morgues. We had to cruise several times past other mangled damaged ships beyond count. We had tried to protect ourselves and our ship from not only suicide planes with bombs but also from suicide swimmers and one-man suicide submarines. Although battered, our own ship was still afloat but with numerous reminders of our lost and injured shipmates. Sitting motionless in the Kerama Retto anchorage for 28 days and to have more future cripples undoubtedly join us was a bleak prospect.

Since we had left Los Angeles toward the end of February and had been underway most of the time since then, the crew had had no opportunity to use the 700 cases of beer locked away for the crew to use in future "Rest and Relaxation Recreation" when conditions would permit. (The inspired officer or officers who made the bargain with the ARL staff are still heroes to the *Purdy* crew.) The arrangement called for the *Purdy* to give the ARL 10 cases of beer for each day they could trim from the projected 28 days. The

Purdy was approved ready to depart in *12 days* (plus time to weld as soon as possible a railroad rail along the port strakes to prevent the *Purdy's* bow from breaking off)

To travel to Guam, a task unit had been formed from a number of various "cripples" including not only the *Purdy* but also three ancient four-stack destroyers, damaged ships of all kinds, the Destroyer *Bryant*, and the remaining 2/3 of the *Lindsey* (DM 33). *Lindsey* had had her bow blown off; she proceeded stern first being also towed backwards by two seagoing tugs. The Convoy got off just before noon on 28 April 1945 heading for Guam, 1200 miles away, at the regal speed of four knots!

All seemed routine until about 2100 hours when we were surprised to see five miles away a brightly lit ship overtaking us. Just as we were about to warn it away from our convoy of cripples, our combat information center detected an unidentified plane closing on the bright ship and then there was a huge explosion. It was our hospital ship *Comfort* and it needed help; it had been hit by a suicide bomber smashing several operating rooms with much damage and many casualties. By radio its Captain asked whether it should darken ship. Our Commodore said to do so at once and sent one of our destroyers to assist. (The flagrant breaking of the Geneva Convention angered and saddened us as we continued our journey to Guam and to Pearl Harbor.) The Commodore was continually pushing the tugs and *Lindsey* for more speed and finally we made 8 knots.

At Pearl Harbor there were orders calling for a Junior Officer to train to become a Torpedo Officer. It was my lot to be chosen and I spent two weeks at Torpedo School in Pearl Harbor while the *Purdy* continued on to reach San Francisco on the 28th of May to go to the Matson Line Piers for major repairs. The unexpected interlude between Okinawa and Pearl Harbor had been relaxing and easy. We had no galley but lots of Orations. Yet we kept thinking not only of our dead and wounded shipmates but also of those on the water, on the land and in the air still fighting to win the war.

After my torpedo school I was fortunate to get a ride on a PB4Y Flying Boat for a 14 hour flight to San Francisco to rejoin the *Purdy*.

We worked hard, as did the Matson line staff to get our ship back to full efficiency. I also had a short leave to Massachusetts. We were practicing shore bombardment off the island of San Clemente when VJ day was announced on August 15, 1945.

Captain Johnson and Executive Officer Davenport had been transferred. Our new Captain was Wilson G. Reifenrath, a top skipper and an excellent ship handler. Our good Gunnery Officer, Tom Turner, was promoted to Executive Officer.

However, we were to go west again: On 20 August 1945 we set off for occupation duty in Japan. After stopping in Pearl Harbor it was on to Tokyo Bay reaching it on 17 October 1945 just missing a floating mine as we entered the harbor. Several of our rifle marksmen kept shooting and finally after 15 shots they blew it up safely.

We spent some seven months moving mail back and forth and providing a "Presence". The Plain of Tokyo was a despairing mess of burned buildings, many smashed ships were on the bottom of the bay. Hiroshima was a desert and we knew little as yet about its horrible after effects. A powerful typhoon visited the area while we were at sea. An unusual snap roll and a big wave crashed against our motor whale boat, pulling it free of its king pins. (We needed a boat to moor to buoys and luckily our Navy planners had an extra one in stock in Yokasuka.)

The few Japanese people we encountered were also tired of war and behaved very well. But we were wary for many months. During this period we had many changes in personnel as many of our shipmates accumulated "points" sufficient to send them home. On the way back from Japan we were assigned several times to the tests of atomic bombs at the Bikini Atoll with its radiation dangers. Fortunately, we were just as often "unassigned"!

Experienced Lew Helphand, our fine deck officer and damage control officer, had returned home. So I had to take the First Lieutenant's tasks. We mercifully made it through the Panama Canal and returned in June to our home port of Boston. In a few days I too was discharged, bidding a mixed goodbye to my "home" for almost two years. Again quoting from Folden's History:

"To the survivors the Purdy *was a lucky ship—after one hit there were no more enemy planes in our vicinity to attack us. No Baka Bombs were in our vicinity although one sank the Abele on Picket Station #20 only 20 miles west of our position. Some minor fires broke out but were extinguished by punctures in the steam lines caused by shrapnel from the exploding shell. Boilers in the forward fire room were secured so we had to operate on boilers 3+4 only, which would have greatly reduced our maximum speed."*

As the war had worn on, it was important not to let the Japanese Military know of how many causalities we had suffered from their Kamikaze attacks. We didn't publish very much in the papers and much was secret. Bill Sholin took the pains in his two books to tally especially how many destroyers and destroyer types were affected by the "The Divine Wind". His book, *The Sacrificial Lambs—U.S. Destroyers vs. Japanese Kamikazes, 1989* included just the U.S. destroyer types. At Okinawa: 148 destroyers took part in the Okinawa campaign. Kamikazes crashed into 119 of them and among these which were hit, 43 were sunk or scrapped. In other words, of the destroyer type vessels in the Battle of Okinawa 80% were crashed by Kamikaze planes and 29% of the total of destroyer types involved were either sunk or had to be scrapped. No wonder, as Sholin notes: "The traumatic effect of experiencing those events is apparent at ships' (crews') reunions, more than 50 years later."

How then to evaluate the Okinawa campaign overall? Robert Leckie in his book, *Okinawa—The Last Battle of World War Two,* summed it up this way:

"The last of the kamikaze had been shot down, the Japanese Thirty-second Army was no more, with roughly 100,000 dead, and, surprisingly, another 10,000 captured. American casualties totaled 49,151, with Marine losses at 2,938 dead or missing and 13,708 wounded; the Army's at 4,675 and 18,099; and the Navy's at 4,907 and 4,824. There was little left of Japanese airpower after losses of about 3,000 planes—about 1,900 of them kamikaze—against 763 for the Americans; and the sinking of Yamato *and 15 other ships meant the end of Nippon's Navy."*

But this gets us into other subjects and questions, the USS *Purdy* DD734 continued on for a lengthy career, going around the world, putting out a fire in a Greek town and serving in the Korean war. It had smaller crews which continued to change in personnel gradually. Finally in 1972/73 the *Purdy* was scrapped.

The partial story of the USS *Purdy*, DD734, is dedicated to the memories of the brave shipmates who were killed or wounded on April 12, 1945.

BIBLIOGRAPHY:

Folden, Ira W.: *A Brief History of the USS* Purdy *(DD734)* ; 18 July 1944 to 8 January 1946
Mimeo by author
Leckie, Robert: *Okinawa—The Last Battle of World War II* New York: Viking Penguin, 1995
USS *Purdy* Association, *The* Purdy *Reports* published by Military Locator and Reunion Service, Hickory, North Carolina
Roscoe, Theodore: *United States Destroyer Operations in World War II* Annapolis, Maryland: United States Naval Institute, 1953
Sholin Bill: *The Sacrificial Lambs—U.S. Destroyers vs. Japanese Kamikazes* Bonney Lake, Washington, Mountain View Publishing, 1989
Sholin, Bill: *The Kamikaze Nightmare* Bonney Lake, Washington, Mountain View Publishing, 2000

TO ANY AND ALL SHIPS

Just now and then
when driving late
at night in rain
there comes the slap
of water in the
dark against a
shell of metal
and a whiff of
diesel brings the
midnights back, the
heavy rolling and
the funnels' sigh.

From: The Perfect Destroyer
Stanley Koehler, poet and Destroyer Officer on DD743

1945 U.S.S. Purdy

Bob Grose, 1944

1945

The task force is like "a beautiful painting...almost unreal"

		No. of Planes		U. S. Ships Damaged		
Attack No.	Date	Kamikaze	Other[3]	Sunk	A	B[4]
1	6-7 April	355	341	6	10	7
2	12-13 April	185	195	2	3	6
3	15-16 April	165	150	1	4	2
4	27-28 April	115	100	1	3	1
5	3-4 May	125	110	6	4	2
6	10-11 May	150	125	0	4	0
7	23-25 May	165	150	3	5	1
8	27-29 May	110	100	1	5	2
9	3-7 June	50	40	0	2	1
10	21-22 June	45	40	1	3	1
	TOTAL	1465	1351	21	43	23

3   Data in this column (after No. 2) are estimates.

4   A, scrapped or decommissioned as result of damage, or repairs incomplete at end of war; B, out of action for over 30 days. The complete table, including ships sunk or damaged between *kikusui* attacks and by causes other than air, will be found in my *History of United States Naval Operations in World War II Vol. XIV: Victory in the Pacific* pp. 390-392.

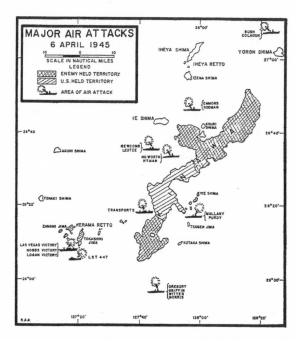

"Ten-Go" Gets Going

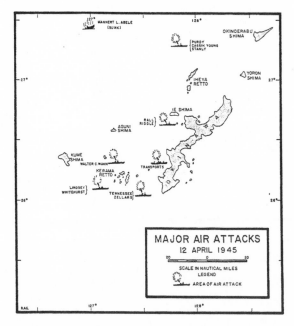

Victory in the Pacific

Excerpts from the "United States Destroyer Operations in World War II " Annapolis, MD, U.S. Naval Institute, 1953

American submarines met practically no opposition. But the destroyer forces on the "Iceberg" front were in there fighting for days and weeks on end. The "small boys" got the man-size job at Okinawa. And they put up a giant-size effort to accomplish that job. The Purdy *was one of the numerous destroyers engaged in that effort.*

Most of the destroyers and destroyer-escorts on the "Iceberg" front worked as radar pickets or patrol vessels in the area screen. Covering the approaches to Okinawa, they mounted guard at radar picket stations positioned in a ring encircling the island, or patrolled the convoy approaches and served as A/S and anti-aircraft guards on a perimeter which embraced the transport area. These picket and patrol ships constituted Task Flotilla 5, under command of a veteran destroyerman, Commodore Frederick Moosbrugger.

The iceberg" mission of the DD's and DE's in Task Flotilla 5 is best detailed in the words of Commodore Moosbrugger, whose official summarization is quoted herewith:

(A) Radar Pickets and Supports.

Distant radar pickets were stationed between 40 and 70 miles from the transport area in the direction of the approach of enemy aircraft from the Japanese Island chain, China bases, and Formosa. Close radar pickets were stationed 20 to 25 miles from the transport area. In addition; stations in the outer and inner anti-submarine screen were designated as radar picket stations. Their special duty consisted of detecting, tracking, and reporting on aircraft in the vicinity of the transport area.

The function of the distant radar pickets was to give early warning of enemy air raids and surface craft, and to perform the duties of fighter direction. Specially equipped fighter-director destroyers with fighter-director teams embarked were used as fighter-director ships. These fighter-director destroyers controlled such units of the CAP as were assigned them by the central fighter-director unit embarked in the ELDORADO *or other headquarters ship. Initially a radar picket group was composed of one FD (fighter-director) destroyer and two*

LCS supports. Each LCS was stationed one-third the distance to an adjacent radar picket station tö increase the probability of detection of low-flying planes and barge or other surface movement along the island chain. In case of attack the supports closed the radar picket for mutual protection. This formation was later-changed, and the LCS's were stationed with the picket as close supports.

The vital importance of maintaining radar picket groups on station can be attested by the fact that the bulk of the defense of the Okinawa amphibious operation evolved around the raid reporting and fighter direction exercised by these exposed fighter-director ships and their supporting elements. It became apparent early in the operation that the brunt of the enemy air attacks would be absorbed by the radar pickets and units of the outer A/S screen, therefore it was considered necessary to increase the number of units on each radar picket station and provide a protective CAP over each radar picket. The possibility of reducing the number of occupied radar picket stations was seriously examined, but the number could not be reduced until after shore based radar stations were in operation.

During the first days of the operation there were insufficient destroyers available to assign more than one destroyer to each occupied picket station. This was occasioned by other required employment such as (1) the necessity of assigning destroyers to screen transport groups, tractor groups, and covering groups in night retirement; (2) assignment of destroyers to task groups in awaiting areas; (3) the necessity of having units available to meet emergencies. However, the strength of the radar picket stations was increased by assigning all available LCS, LSM®, and PGM types as close supports. Later; when night retirement was discontinued and groups returned from awaiting areas, additional destroyers were assigned as radar picket supports. Beginning 10 April it was possible to assign two destroyers and four small picket support craft to the more exposed radar picket stations. Continued damage to units prevented increasing the strength further until reinforcements arrived from other areas and the number of picket stations was reduced. Finally on 19 May it became possible to maintain at least three destroyers and four LCS's on each of the five occupied stations.

Destroyer-escorts and similar type were considered as picket supports. Their inadequate anti-aircraft armament precluded exposing them to the vicious air attacks experienced on radar picket stations. None of the destroyer-escorts with the increased armament of two 5-inch, ten 40 mm. and ten 20 mm. guns were at the objective.

Continued efforts were made to obtain a protective CAP of from four to six planes for each picket station. This special CAP was to be employed solely for local picket protection, reporting directly to the radar picket on a special frequency. It was entirely separate from the regular CAP. Sufficient planes were not available at the objective to supply the desired, protective CAP, but commencing 14 April the TAF (Tactical Air Force) was able to maintain a two-plane protective CAP over three picket stations, and later over five stations.

In the early stages Radar Picket Stations 1, 2, 3, 4, 7, 10, 12, and 14, were filled, with number 9 later when more warning was thought necessary against low-flying planes approaching Kerama Retto from southwest. On 16 May, with the completion of shore-based radar installations on Hedo Saki and Ie Shima, the number of occupied radar picket stations was reduced to five (Stations 5, 7, 9, 15, and 16.)

Due to damage to fighter-director ships it was necessary to continuously equip additional ships with fighter-director radio and associated equipment, and in some ships, not so equipped, with suitable visual fighter-direction stations....

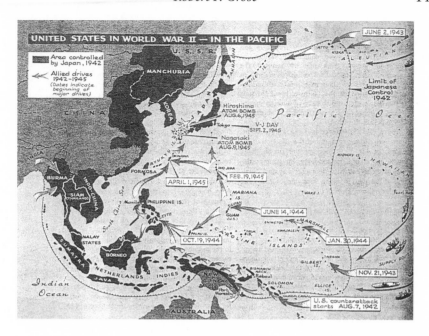

Bob Grose Today

ROBERT W LENZ

Service in the Army Air Corp from June 6, 1944 to November 8, 1945

I enlisted in the Army Air Corp in February 1944, when I was still 17 years old and in my final term in high school. After graduating from high school, which occurred before my 18th birthday, so I could not begin my service, I attended one semester at Brooklyn Polytechnic Institute. Immediately after the semester was completed, which was about one month after my 18th birthday, I began my service at the Army Air Corp induction center at Fort Dix, N.J.. Following several days of "orientation", I was sent by train to Keesler Field in Biloxi, MI, for three months of basic training in things military, including calisthenics, obstacle courses, pistol and rifle training with marksmanship tests, marching drills, poison gas recognition drills, a 20 mile hike with full pack, a variety of lectures and demonstrations, and full dress parades. At the completion of basic, I was transferred to Courtland Air Force Base in Decatur, AL to take a battery of tests to determine which specific area of training I was to receive in the Army Air Corp. I passed the examinations for admission into the Aviation Cadet program, and I was assigned to navigator school at Craig Field in Selma, AL. By then, in November 1944, the Air Corp had so many navigators in the pipeline that they did not know what to do with us, so we did little more than mark time for the next six months. During that period I only flew once ,in a bomber, so to try to do something useful, I applied for admission into the West Point Military Academy. Again, after a battery of mental and physical exams, I was admitted to West Point, and I was scheduled to be transferred there in August 1945. However, the war ended before my shipment date, and everything was put on hold until the Army decided how big a class they wanted to have at the Academy. They apparently decided that they already had enough students for their peace-time needs, so instead of my going to West Point I was discharged "at the convenience of the government" as soon as they could process me out.- In November 1945 I was discharged at Westover Air Force Base, after having fought my war in Mississippi and Alabama, wearing my aviation cadet wings and three ribbons on my uniform dress jacket. The ribbons were for the Good Conduct Medal, the Markmanship Medal and the Victory Medal.

*Robert Lenz as Aviation Cadet, Craig Air
Force Base, Alabama, 1944*

Distinguished Polymer Scientiest Robert Lenz,
University of Massachusetts, 2003

JACK MATHEWS' STORY   B 6/26/26

I was inducted at Fort Banks, Mass., from Worcester, on November 29, 1944. Received equipment and clothing at Fort Devens, then was shipped to Camp Wheeler, near Macon, Georgia, in December.

There I received 15 weeks of infantry basic training. After completion of the cycle I had a two-week delay en route, which gave us a break before reporting to Fort Ord, California.

We boarded the USS *Gov. Mann* in San Francisco for deployment to Manila, This was about an 18-day trip. We were assigned to the 5th Repple Depple (replacement depot) for a short while, then to the 43rd Infantry Division. Fortunately, I was assigned to the 43rd Signal Company, radio operators' school. After four weeks' training, I was able to receive and send 20 words per minute.

The 43rd Division went into rest camp to prepare for the invasion of Kyushu. as part of the Sixth Army. I was one of the radio operators for division headquarters. While in rest camp, the war ended. The 43rd Division, along with others, was deployed to be in the occupation force for Japan. We left in August from Manila, and ran into parts of a typhoon on the way to Yokohama. It was a rough storm.

Our division located its headquarters in Kumagaya, Honshu, Japan. Our radio truck was sent to Yokohama to send and receive messages to division headquarters. Shortly afterwards I was assigned to the 98th Signal Service. From there I went to Choshi, Japan, a fishing village northeast of Tokyo. The army was supervising the dumping of Japanese arms, munitions, bombs and poison gas five miles out to sea. I sent reports of dumpings and weather reports to and from corps headquarters in Yokohama. I had two tours at Choshi.

I had a one-week rest camp at Nikko, well known for its shrines. I did a short stint of teaching at the 3186th Signal Service Battalion. Received orders to return home in October, 1946, and was discharged at Fort Dix, N. J., on November 18.

CHESTER PENZA

Sergeant Chester Penza
United States Army July 9, 1943 to December 28, 1945
Company B Supply Battalion 6th Armored Division 3578 Q M
Truck Company

I graduated from Amherst Regional High School in Amherst, MA on June 23, 1943, and the next day was inducted into the United States Army. I was ordered to report for duty to Fort Devens in Massachusetts on July 9, 1943.

I received training at the following camps and forts: Camp Grant - Illinois, Camp Cooke - California, Camp Young - California, Fort Fisher - North Carolina, and Fort Dix - New Jersey.

On May 10, 1944, I along with 8000 G I's left the New York Port of Embarkation on the British Ship SS *Andes* and arrived in England on May 18, 1944. In England we picked up all our vehicles at different depots and moved to the Southampton Bournemouth area. There we learned how to waterproof our vehicles in preparation for a landing in France.

In June of 1944, I landed on Omaha Beach in France, and participated in the following campaigns; Normandy, Northern France, Rhineland, Ardennes and Central Europe. Our main task throughout all the campaigns was to transport troops, ammunition, gasoline, rations and German prisoners of war. When the war ended on May 8, 1945, I was in Regensburg, Germany. After several days, our company was ordered to travel to Frankfort, Germany where we were assigned the task of providing transportation for SHAEF

Headquarters. A short time later the name of the headquarters was changed to USFET Headquarters.

On December 2, 1945, I along with 580 other G I's left Antwerp Belgium on the converted Liberty Ship the SS *John Cropper*. After a very rough crossing, I landed in Hampton Rhodes, Virginia, on December 25, 1945.

On Christmas Day, (Dec. 25, 1945) I boarded a train to Fort Devens, Massachusetts, where I was processed and received my Honorable Discharge from the United States Army, on December 28, 1945.

I received from the Army, the following decorations & citations: European African Middle Eastern Theater Campaign Ribbon, Good Conduct Medal, Motor Vehicles Drivers Award, and the Victory Medal.

Editor's note: Chet Penza landed on Omaha beach in mid-June, 1944, only days after "the longest day," June 6, 1944. As a member of the United States Army Transportation Corps, he helped secure the beachead and to supply the troops who were advancing through France toward Germany. He eventually arrived at Regensburg, Germany, where he was stationed when V-E day was declared. After landing at Normandy just following "D-Day," Penza proceeded across Europe through France, Belgium, Luxembourg, and finally Germany. The 3758 QuarterMaster Truck Company crossed the Rhine River into Cologne, Germany, and proceeded south toward Frankfurt, then further south to Regensburg. The photograph on the following page is exactly what Chet Penza saw on his arrival at Normandy in June, 1944.

Omaha beach: supplies pour off the transport ships.

Penza during the occupation in 1945.

Chet Penza in Basic Training, Camp

Honorable Discharge

This is to certify that

CHESTER PENZA 31 348 626 SERGEANT

COMPANY B SUPPLY BATTALION 6TH ARMORED DIVISION
Army of the United States

is hereby Honorably Discharged from the military service of the United States of America.

This certificate is awarded as a testimonial of Honest and Faithful Service to this country.

Given at   SEPARATION CENTER
FORT DEVENS MASS

Date   28 DECEMBER 1945

Chet Penza, 2001

On Furlough in October, 1943

*Chet Penza in May,
1944, prior to overseas
assignment Offenbach,
Germany, Fall, 1945*

*Offenbach, Germany,
Fall, 1945*

THE COMMONWEALTH OF
MASSACHUSETTS

IN RECOGNITION OF THE SERVICE OF

Chester Penza

IN THE ARMED FORCES OF THE
UNITED STATES OF AMERICA

PRESENTS THIS TESTIMONIAL
OF ESTEEM AND GRATITUDE FOR
FAITHFUL PERFORMANCE
OF DUTIES IN

WORLD WAR II

DONALD R. PROGULSKE

USNR, 8251475

PRE-MILITARY

Born 9/3/23 in Springfield, Massachusetts where I grew up and graduated from Springfield Technical High School in January, 1941 when the United States was becoming increasingly involved in supporting Great Britain and her allies in Europe, I immediately began work as an apprentice machinist in a manufacturing plant producing gyroscopic ship compasses and special shell loading machines. The entire industrial complex of the country was beginning to produce war materials when the military draft, initiated in October, 1940, took thousands of young men from crucial industries. After agreeing to accept "industrial deferments" for nine months to help the war effort I decided I'd try to enlist in naval service. A new Navy College training program (V-12) had just been announced; I was fortunate (having no college prep courses) to pass the entrance exam and was assigned to Harvard University where I reported on July 1, 1943.

MILITARY SERVICE

Navy Training Unit at Harvard University; 7/1/43 - 6/15/44
Completed three academic semesters concentrating on engineering subjects

Navy Training Center, Sampson, NY; 6/15/44 - 10/24/44
Regular basic training; awaited entrance to a service school

Naval Training Station, Newport, RI; 10/30/43 - 1/8/44
    Ships Company with kitchen duties in mess hall
Naval Distribution Center, Camp Shoemaker, CA; 1/12/44 -
    1/20/44
    Awaited assignment for sea duty
Naval Magazine, Port Chicago, CA; 1/20/44 - 5/2/46
    Loading of ammunition then a base photographer for
    four months prior to my discharge
Naval Ammunition Depot, Mare Island, CA; two weeks
    special training in above period
Treasure Island Separation Center, Treasure Island, CA
    then Separation Center , Boston. Honorable Discharge,
    Seaman 1C on 5/10/46.

PORT CHICAGO NAVAL MAGAZINE
—A UNIQUE FACILITY

I present this following brief history of the base because it relates to a memorable event I experienced there.

On December 9, 1941, two days after Japan attacked Pearl Harbor, authorization was given to construct the magazine on the Sacramento River approximately 30 miles from San Francisco.. The facility was the first pier in U.S. history built for loading and transshipping ammunition and high explosives. It served as the main naval facility for the war with Japan. Construction was completed and the first ship sailed from there with her dangerous cargo in September 1942. The station consisted of a Tidal and Inland Area, connected by a government-owned railroad and military highway. Seventy-one white officers were put in charge of over 1,400 black untrained navymen who loaded ammunition aboard transport ships in three around-the-clock seven-hour shifts. At that time the Navy did not allow black men to enter combat, nor were blacks commissioned as Navy officers. White marines secured the base and coastguard men patrolled the water areas.

On July 17, 1944 two ships were being loaded at the pier, one for her maiden voyage; the other had just returned from her first voyage. The holds of both vessels were packed with bombs, high explosives, ammunition, and depth charges, totaling 4,607 tons. Between the two ships 16 railcars on the pier contained another 429 tons of munitions. At 0:18 pm a tragic super explosion of the cargo occurred and 320 men working on the pier were killed instantly, including 202 black enlisted men. Additionally, 390 other military and civilian personnel were injured.

The day after the explosion the surviving black navymen on the base were sent to another close by station for reassignment; some were transferred to Mare Island Munitions Depot and many back to Port Chicago. In the aftermath of the disaster, on August 9, 1944, most refused to work with munitions. Unfortunately this led to the largest mass trial in U.S. Navy history; 258 men were imprisoned then brought to a lengthy trial. Fifty leaders of the action were sentenced to 15 years in prison while all the others were court-martialed. Several months hence, the Navy abandoned its skewed racial policy and brought the first white dock workers on board to load ships on the same twenty-four hour schedule indicated above. I was among them and was assigned to work on the pier for several months then in the Inland Area.

Located three miles southwest of the Tidal area, the Inland Area, covering several square miles, included 171 storage magazines and several testing buildings. Shipments of ammunition and high explosives were brought in by rail or truck. Those of us working there were given training in handling ammunition, depth charges, large bombs, etc. with custom-made machines. Work in the Area was restricted to daylight hours because electricity was banned and even during thunderstorms we had to secure the bunker and vacate to the barracks. Needless to say, work in the Inland Area was more bearable than that on the pier.

One late afternoon in mid-July (1945), while working in one of the bunkers, I and two other co-workers were directed by our officer in charge to go to the Tidal Area for an early supper then come back for a special detail. Upon returning we were taken to a bunker where a couple of marines stood guard in the presence of three or four base officers. We were told to load the unusual heavy wood-crated items, perhaps 15 to 20, into the truck at the bunker dock. The work took less than an hour, the bunker was closed, and we were released for the day. I thought little of the incident at the time; it became more meaningful before long!

As we know, on August 6 the first uranium bomb, "Little Boy" was released over Hiroshima and the plutonium bomb "Fat Boy" was dropped on Nagasaki on August 9. The next day Japan sued for peace, bringing end to all hostilities in the Pacific. On September 2, 1945 Japanese Emperor Hirohito signed the surrender document aboard the USS *Missouri* and all branches of the U.S. military began returning unneeded personnel to civilian life. Soon after the Navy Command commended personnel at Port Chicago Magazine for having an important role in sending components of the atomic bomb(s) to the South Pacific for assembly. I felt I had a small part in that historic event when I help load those crated items for transshipment in 1945.

Port Chicago Naval Magazine was designated a National Memorial (National Park Service) on July 17, 1992 fifty years after the disasterous explosion to honor the courage and commitment of the 320 Sailors, Marines, Coast Guardsmen, Merchant Mariners, and civilians killed there. It was dedicated by survivors in 1994. The tragedy and its aftermath influenced the U.S. Navy and other military branches to address racial injustice and strive for equality following WWII.

POST-MILITARY SERVICE

Separation from military service was according to points accumulated for total time in service and overseas duty. My turn for separation began May 1, 1946 and I was actually discharged from the Fargo Building in Boston on May 10, having served just short of three years.

Upon being released from the Navy Reserve, I signed up for the "20-52 club", a program designed to help discharged military personnel adjust to civilian life and employment. Veterans could draw $20/

month for 52 weeks. Being unsure of my career aims, I found this
helpful for several weeks before I returned to my former machinist
job for one year then decided to attend college under the "GI Bill"
. The three semesters of courses at Harvard University enabled me
to complete a BS Degree in Wildlife Management at the University
of Massachusetts in 1950. Then in sequence I earned an MS Degree
in Wildlife and Forestry at Virginia Polytech Institute in 1952 and a
PhD in Zoology at the University of Missouri in 1956. I immediately
joined the faculty at South Dakota State University and later was
appointed Head of the Wildlife and Fisheries Science department
until 1972 when I accepted the headship of the Forestry and Wildlife
Management Department at the University of Massachusetts. In 1981
I relinquished administration in favor of teaching and research then
retired in 1990. Whatever success I achived was largely because of
the solid support my wife, Eunice (an RN), gave me during all the
years since our wedding in 1947, especially when rearing our two
daughters and two sons, now all college educated and married with
a total of eight children.

Donald Proguiske today. Seen here with Rotarians
Stan Ziomek and Gerry Whitlock (deceased) at
Rotary sponsored Amherst Town Fair, 1995.

Proguiske and Fellow Amherst Rotarian and
WWII Veteran Dunc Fraser, 2000

1943, in full Navy dress blues.

A recent picture

ARTHUR R. QUINTON

Sub-Lieutenant RNVR 1944-46

At the Teheran Conference, Roosevelt, Churchill and Stalin mapped out the grand strategy for bringing the war in Europe to a victorious end. There would be two invasions: one launched from Britain across the English Channel and a second from the Mediterranean into the South of France. The Italian Campaign was already well underway.

Churchill was not a supporter of the plan to take on the German Army at Provence and suggested alternatives. But Roosevelt and Marshall insisted, mainly it seems, because that was what had been promised Stalin! I joined a ship, FDT13, just after she had taken part in "Operation Dragoon", the code-name for the South of France invasion. She was at the time in the London Graving Dock, undergoing a refit for the Pacific War.

In the planning for the invasions a specific problem was quickly anticipated. For the airwar over Britain, the RAF had developed a very successful system of control of fighters from the ground. Radar was used to track all aircraft with friend and foe separately identified by the so-called IFF[5] system. Ground-based controllers were then able to direct the fighters, via radio contact, to engage the enemy aircraft by providing them with the necessary information for a favorable intercept. The problem was that any invasion site, for example Normandy, would be outside the range of both the radar and radio transmitters for effective control. It would have to be done from ships in the invasion fleet instead of from airfields

5   IFF stands for Interrogation (or Identification) of Friend or Foe

or other ground based control centers, at least until a secure beach-head was established.

The problem was tackled by the acquisition of three LST's from the United States. In the hands of the John Brown Shipyards on the Clyde in Scotland they were converted into Fighter Direction Tenders or FDT's. These ships without names were FDT13, FDT216 and FDT217. Initially RAF crews were responsible for the mainte-nance of the radar and radio communications equipment. The Royal Navy manned the ships while because of their prior experience RAF officers worked as controllers in the operations rooms.

The first full scale test ended in disaster. FDT 217 was assigned to join a mock American invasion force off the Dorset coast in "Operation Tiger". Before she could arrive, German E-boats from Cherbourg created havoc among the landing craft. The Royal Navy had failed to provide the necessary protective shield due to a com-munications failure. FDT 217 was turned back just in time to avoid certain disaster.

But D-Day June 6th,1944 was another story. The three FDT's were positioned off the Normandy beaches and carried out their assign-ments with complete success. Equipment to establish land-based fighter control was damaged during the landings and consequently the ships were on station for nearly three weeks. Unfortunately during this time FDT216 was hit by a torpedo from a Junkers 88 and had to be sunk. A little later FDT13 was sent to the Mediterranean in support of the American 7th Army, under General Patch, for the successful invasion of the French Riviera (August 15th, 1944). She was in the Adriatic at the time of the liberation of Greece. Making her way home via the port of Bizerta the vessel experienced engine troubles. The fuel oil had been contaminated, probably as a result of sabotage.

I was a twenty year old, very raw sublieutenant when naval trans-port deposited me and my gear on the quay where FDT13 was tied up in the London Graving Dock. I first asked my new shipmates if "FDT" had a meaning. "Oh yes!" came the reply "Floating Death Trap!" Most of the officers were also RNVR. The captain however was RNR because of his professional status in the mercantile marine, as first mate on the *Queen Mary* I was told. There were five RAF officers, all experienced in fighter control in contrast to the RNVR controllers who were new to the game. Lieutenant Gillies, the radar officer, had seen invasion action, as had the Chief Engineer. All the rest of us had recently joined the ship. Gillies befriended me to some degree. He soon succeeded in convincing the authorities that he was psychologically unfit for further duties. His replacement was as inexperienced as I.

All the RAF maintenance technical staff had left the ship and replaced by naval ratings from Devonport. The control room wiring had been ripped out and there were no circuit diagrams available. A Scottish engineer from the Dockyard and I set about the job of getting the equipment back in order. There was also one new petty officer who knew enough to be helpful.

In preparation for service in the Far East the ship's ventilation system was being improved. On the technical side, a new radar was installed. The replaced radar had been designed to work on the frequency used by the German radar. It had been correctly assumed that the enemy would not jam its own equipment during the invasions. The GCI (Ground Controlled Interception) antenna, the workhorse for fighter control, was retained. This large rotating structure had worked surprisingly well, even when there were heavy seas.

My main responsibility was the communications equipment. I had seen some of the receivers during my training course as a midshipman at Portsmouth. But most of the equipment was new to me, although the transmitters were similar to several others on which I had worked. These transmitters were manufactured in the USA and no doubt made available to Britain as part of the Lend-Lease Agreement.

I was agreeably surprised to find that my training at Cambridge and on HMS *Mercury* was general enough so that I was able to cope with the situation. In any case, like so many wartime experiences there was no choice! Actually there were two petty officers on my staff. One of them was in the navy as a career. He let me know very quickly that he knew nothing on the technical side but that he could take care of the wireless operators. So he did that and I did not have to spend time on that duty at all. Occasionally I would need someone to climb a mast in order to fix a dipole antenna and he would recruit the volunteer for that job, for example. The second petty officer worked with me on the ship-to-air transmitters and that turned out to be an excellent arrangement. There were no egos involved, his practical skills complemented my theory and we got the job done. If a fault came on a transmitter we could look at meter readings and examine circuit diagrams and make guesses as to the component at fault. He would then get to work and in no time flat we would be back on the air. There were a dozen of these crystal controlled transmitters. Given the frequency of the day for ship-to-air communication, we could tune each set to full power in a matter of a few minutes. Except for the anticipated trip to Davy Jones Locker we were ready to take on the Japanese Air Force!

It was a proud moment for me when we left the Thames for the open seas. We sailed around the south coast of England and into the Irish Sea where we enjoyed some shore-leave at Douglas in the Isle of Man. There was no ship-to-air activity during this trip but I did get a call from the captain to report to the bridge. He wanted me to check out the conventional direction finding equipment. Yet another fast learning experience for me since I had never seen this equipment before! I presume that this trip into the Irish Sea was designed to check out the ship as a seagoing vessel rather than as a fighter direction tender. But this was about to change.

Now we were headed for warmer waters as we rolled our way across the Bay of Biscay to Gibraltar where we switched to tropical uniforms. In the Mediterranean we proceeded to the naval base at Valetta in Malta. The opportunity had been taken to take part in training operations with an RAF squadron , presumably based in Italy. l was delighted and surprised to find that all the communications equipment that was my responsibility worked well.

By now it was August 1945. One day we learned that the United States Army Air Corps had dropped a new type of bomb on the city of Hiroshima. Shortly after, a second bomb was dropped on Nagasaki and within days the war was over. I do not recall that we switched the transmitters on again. All training exercises came to an end and we awaited our next orders. Meanwhile we celebrated often with shore-leave in the bright lights of downtown Valetta in civilian clothes. Fortunately for me the Chief Engineer took me under his wing and saw to it that I came to no lasting harm.

With no technical duties to speak of, I was enjoying the life of a tourist until the First Lieutenant, a rather fierce disciplinarian with a CID (Scotland Yard) background, thought up a new duty for me. Under normal circumstances only the deck officers, sometimes called the executive branch, were assigned the duty of officer-of the-day. But in port we technical types were given this duty. With the help of a very friendly chief petty officer, the master-of-arms of the ship, I managed to get by although completely unprepared as far as training was concerned. An especially important duty involved the supervision of the rum ration issue with the aforementioned CPO, at noon each day, after the piping of "rum up"!

Eventually we received orders to return to the UK. The first port of call was Greenock on the Clyde Estuary where I recall seeing the *Queen Mary* by then presumably returning GI's back to the States. But most of the winter was spent at Inveraray on Loch Fyne, the home of "Combined Operations" of which we were told we were a part. Recently (2003) I learned that some sort of monument is planned there in order to commemorate the contributions of those special forces who took part in such raids as Bruneval and Dieppe.

Then with a skeleton crew we left Scotland to return to the London Graving Dock. Our splendid equipment was removed and I understand eventually it ended up in a dump. I was sent home on indefinite leave. FDT13 was later returned to the US Navy at Norfolk, Virginia and struck from the Navy's lists. In late 1947 she was sold to Luria Brothers & Co.,lnc. for scrap. Since she had been launched in January 1943 at the shipyards of the Dravo Corporation in Pittsburgh it is estimated that she was in service for 1870 days.[6]

After a while I tired of indefinite leave. So I wrote to the Commanding Officer at HMS *Mercury*, the Royal Navy's Signal School, with a request for a new assignment. In short order I found myself on the north coast of Cornwall, at the Royal Naval Air Station,

---

6   Go to search engine Google and search on "FDT13" or "Combinedops"

St. Merryn (HMS *Vulture*). Here the surviving aces of the Fleet Air Arm had been assembled to form the School of Naval Air Warfare. At long last the Fairey Swordfish biplanes had been replaced with Barracudas and these higher performance aircraft required new flying tactics to be worked out. My immediate superior was the Marquis of Milford Haven who, following the tradition of his uncle Lord Louis Mountbatten, had entered the navy as a cadet and was by now an RN signals officer. Later he became famous not for his naval achievements but because he was the best man at Philip and Elizabeth's wedding.

My duties, like those of Lt. Milford Haven, were not well defined. There was some equipment at the end of runways, associated with landing in bad weather, and this required some attention. But my main memory is that of ensuring that our work area was shipshape so that as the Commander approached on his rounds, I was able to salute and report "W/T workshop ready for your inspection, Sir!" More significantly I spent lots of liberty time on the south coast of Cornwall where I met my wife-to-be. November 16th 1946 was an auspicious day. Not only was I "demobbed" but I also married Rose Maud Trebilcock of St. Blazey Gate, Cornwall.

Allen Torrey, Arthur Quinton, Connie Wogrin 2003

*Arthur Quinton as
Royal Naval Officer*

Arthur Quinton Today

*Arthur Quinton,
His Majesty's Royal
Navy, 1944.*

*Quinton in second from
left in group photo*

TOM QUARLES SERVICE IN WORLD WAR II

Unites States Naval Reserves

In 1944, I was enrolled as a civilian undergraduate student at Yale University. I was in the middle of my junior year. Before completing that semester, on April 25, 1944, I traveled to New York city and at 33 Pine Street, the Naval Reserve Office for officer training, I volunteered. I passed the requisite medical exam and enlisted in the Navy V-5 aviation training program.

I was instructed to return to my studies at Yale and they would contact me when ready to induct me into active service. I finished my semester studies in late spring, 1944, and anticipating a call from the Navy, left college and returned to my New Jersey home. It was a long wait. On September 6, 1944, I was inducted into active service in the Navy at a ceremony in New York City together with approximately fifteen other men as Seaman, Second Class. We inductees traveled by train from New York City to Memphis, Tennessee. We were then bused to the U.S. Naval Air Station at Willington, Tenn. There we received our uniforms, our bed assignments in the barracks, and under the supervision of a chief Petty Officer, we learned how to live and serve as Second Class Seamen(one step up from the bottom rung of apprentice seaman).

The Naval Air Station at Willington was a Primary Flight Training facility for Naval Aviation cadets. The training aircraft was the Stearman NTS, a single prop biplane with two cockpits and dual controls. It was given the nickname of "yellow Peril" because of the color. (see photo in Allen Torrey account, where the Stearman biplane was also used in training). The cadet occupied the front cockpit and the officer-instructor occupied the rear one. Verbal communication was achieved through a tube named a "gosport " Our duties at the flight line(tarmac) were to inspect the aircraft for safety features, and pull out the wheel blocks when the plane was ready to go to the runway for takeoff. In addition we did wind-tee duty at outlying fields where cadets practiced take-offs and landings.

In early November, 1944, we left the NAS Wellington and boarded a troop train at Memphis which took us to Oakland, California. Even traveling day and night, it took three days to reach our destination. It was a fine trip, following for a great part, the Santa Fe rail line. Our first stop was Amarillo, Texas, then on to New Mexico and Arizona with beautiful sights of the Painted Desert. At Oakland, we were bussed to the N.S. Navy Pre-Flight School at St. Mary's College in the Moraga Valley east of Berkeley, California. This relatively small Catholic College was taken over by the Navy for its West coast Pre-Flight School. The college was in a lovely setting and here we traded our seaman sailor uniforms for the uniforms, both work and dress, of Naval Aviation Cadets. It was quite a step up!! Our daily schedule as cadets was basically class work in the mornings, athletics in the afternoon, and study and sleep at night. Class work was heavy on navigation, recognition of friendly and foe aircraft, current events and reasons for fighting the axis powers. After lunch, we even had instruction in relaxation on the bunk beds!

Saturday mornings, we had inspection, both of the rooms and our persons. If one had no demerits, liberty was available by bus to Berkeley and thence to San Francisco and the Bay area. Liberty ended at 8 p.m. on Sunday night. If one was confined to the campus or chose not to leave over the weekend, there were athletic contests (touch football games) on Saturday and Sunday afternoons. On Saturday nights, the Navy Band(military during the day) became a wonderful swing band and young ladies from the Bay area were bussed to the gym on the base where dancing and socializing took place easily. The band members, mostly African-American, were in civilian life members of top swing bands of the era: Count Basie, Duke Ellington, etc.

The normal time for Cadets at the Pre-Flight School was three months. We were "ninety —day wonders," as career officers used to scoff. Because the pipe line for naval aviators was backing up, we stayed at St. Mary's College for six months. We were certainly over-trained by the end of our second "ninety days." Finally, our pre-flight training was completed and all cadets were given leave of three to four weeks so we could return to our homes. I went to the nearby Alameda Naval Air Station and hooked a ride on a Marine paratroop plane headed for Jacksonville, Florida. It was a C-47(DC-3) twin engine but had no lights so we could not fly at night. The first night, we stopped at NAS Omaha, Nebraska. The second night, we stopped at NAS Columbus, Ohio. I left the plane there and took the train the rest of the way to my New Jersey home.

After the long leave, my orders were to report to the US Naval Air Station, Ottawa, Iowa, where I arrived in May of 1945. Here, we started primary flight training in the NTS "Yellow Perils" which we first encountered in Tennessee. Primary training was divided into stages. "A" Stage was the solo flight. I had a good instructor and after the given number of dual flights, I was able to pass my solo flight test. We were given log books to keep the record of our days and times in the air. "B" stage was for take offs and landings at outlying fields. "C" stage consisted of aerobatics and was great fun. That's when I learned to stall the plane and to go into a tail-spin or free fall and then kick out of the spin while restarting the engine. We also learned to fly the biplane upside down, and all sorts of aerobatic maneuvers such as the Emmelman turn. "D" Stage was formation flying with other planes. It was at this stage that I began to throw up my stomach contents while flying. I was put into the sick bay where doctors tired to determine my problem. Eventually, it turned out that I was anemic with a red blood cell count of less than one million and hemoglobin too low to read.

I was flown by hospital plane to Glenview Naval Air Station north of Chicago and then by ambulance to Great Lakes Naval Hospital. Here, I was subject to some of the best medical personnel in our out of the military. It was determined that I did not have either leukemia or aplastic anemia. The diagnosis then turned to pernicious anemia. My treatment was high protein diet and injections of liver extract. While I was still confined to my hospital bed, V-E day was declared. After my condition stabilized and I was once more mobile, I had only to be present at my bedside each morning right after breakfast for a cursory attendance and medical checkup. After that, I was free to go where I wanted and there was no curfew for checking into the hospital at night. My doctors informed me that because of my anemia, I would not be allowed to resume my flight training. They had already forwarded papers to Washington, D.C.,. for my eventual medical discharge.

BOB SHUMWAY'S STORY   B 2/20/24

My final days at Williston Academy were interrupted by a call from the office of the commanding general of the Army Ground Forces. My first assignment at Camp Edwards was serving with an anti-aircraft artillery unit getting ready for overseas duty in a few weeks. I was ill prepared for this change in my life. From prep school to combat!

But I had seen a poster on the bulletin board that said, "Applications now being accepted for aviation cadet training—we need pilots now!" So I took the exam and was accepted immediately. The anti-aircraft artillery unit to which I had first assigned was already on the high seas. Bob Page, an Amherst Pelham resident, who was a member of that antiaircraft group, was killed in the first three weeks of action.

I had Air Force basic training at Greensboro, N. C., then on to Santa Anna Army Air Base, California, for pilot pre-flight training. I thought I had found my niche in life but it was to end all too soon. Thousands of Army Specialized Training Corps trainees, and aviation cadets in advanced pilot training, who had originally been in the ground forces, cadets who had originally been in the ground troops were being hurriedly transferred to the infantry.

I was off to Camp Roberts, California, in the mountains with the 89th Division, then to Camp Buttner, North Carolina. After obstacle courses, infiltration courses and bayonet drill, we shipped out to Camp Myles Standish in Massachusetts. During our six days at Myles Standish, I had a 12-hour pass. I went to Boston, called home and met a relative. I left him my only piece of equity—a gold watch. On January 10, 5,400 men of the 89th Division were given hot coffee and donuts from Red Cross girls, and stepped up the gang plank with one thought in mind—is this trip necessary? Soon we were in convoy on the high seas. From time to time our escorting destroyers dropped depth charges, and then we were scared to death.

We landed in Le Havre in zero weather. We dug trenches in case of possible enemy air attacks. Large areas of towns we saw had been leveled and the homes which still stood were often shells of walls. Once we located two fields containing over a thousand land mines. It was here that I witnessed my first casualty.

We were eventually assigned to General Patton's Third Army. I carried a BAR—a Browning Automatic Rifle—and I will tell you sometimes there were not enough bullets coming out of that barrel. My closest friend was wounded the second day out and I was terrified.

After taking Hontheim, Wispelt and Krukhof, we had the Germans backing up to the Moselle River. The fighting here was intense. We were strafed by Fock Wolfe 109s, pounded by 88s, mortars and machine guns at the river bank in Ernst as we crossed in our assault boats. We moved in behind tanks—the tankers would throw us an occasional loaf of bread.

The crossing of the Rhine River at Oberwesel was another catastrophic event. The vineyards on the river bank were great hiding places for the Germans, who opened up machine gun and 20-mm fire at us. We had taken a prisoner at night and we could not silence him. One of our men took the liberty of bayoneting him. A ghastly sight.

In 28 days, our outfit headed the Third Army in river crossings. We were then given three days to catch up on a much needed rest. Next we advanced eastward toward Eisenach and the autobahn (the turnpike or super highway). The panzer divisions and German planes were giving us hell. Most of us jumped in the river and backtracked as fast as we could with shells landing all over. I don't know how we survived that one. Our reconnaissance people had goofed—it was later that we found out we shouldn't have been there at this time. I was never so close to hedges and ditches. They were our means of survival.

At Ohrdruf we liberated one of the largest concentration camps, where the SS had just fled from the scene. An estimated 9,000 decomposed bodies were there including an American pilot. He had been shot and was lying on a stretcher. I have pictures of this.

The Germans were pulling back quickly now but we still met stiff resistance in Zwichau, the largest city so far. Sniper fire was our worst enemy. I can remember a time when the food supply was so low I had one can of Spam for two days. Wouldn't a McDonalds taste good at this time? Later we broke into a house and found a whole crate of eggs in the cellar. I cooked and ate 18 of them.

Toward the end of April prisoners were turning up everywhere and we were moving at a great pace. The 89th Division, in order to replace its losses, joined the 83rd Division. In Zwickau, we finally ran into the Russians. C and K rations were issued. On April 28 we enjoyed our first hot meal prepared from A rations (fresh food)even though it wasn't exactly like your mother's turkey dinner. We got the word from headquarters that the war had ended. VE Day was May 8, although the surrender did not become official until one minute past midnight May 9.

It was occupation time. Offers to some of us to extend our time in OCS were declined, I had had enough. Point systems were used at the cigarette camps for being discharged and sent home. In the meantime, I took many passes to Paris, Brussels, Garmische and three weeks in the United Kingdom and Scotland. Saw my first opera in Vienna, Austria.

As for the scars and memories, I received a combat infantry badge, a 10% disability benefit for life. It took time for me to rid myself psychologically of the hatred I had toward the Germans— and I'm part German. I cannot believe I ever went through this ordeal, and may my son or your son never have this experience. It is part of my life that no longer feels real to me.

(It is 80 degrees down here in Florida today. Have a good winter!)
Robert L. Shumway Formerly 89th Division

Written January, 1995

At Ohrdruf, the 355ᵗʰ Regiment which I was a member captured the largest concentration camp liberated by American forces. This had been a German OCS training center. According to prisoner accounts the occupants of the camp, mostly slave laborers from Eastern Europe, had been starved and beaten to death, or shot down at the whim of their SS overseers. Men who had died in the camp had been buried in a huge common pit. When news came of our approach, belated attempts were made to cover up the horrors of the place.

Just before our arrival the SS guards machine-gunned the prisoners too ill to walk and had fled. Included among the dead, shot in the courtyard when we entered was the body of an American flyer. He was shot as he lay on a stretcher.

When the German personnel in charge of the camp fled in terror a German ex-convict who was employed as a ward boss at the camp stayed behind. He estimated the number of men buried in the common pit at 9000. Shortly after our arrival the Burgermeister of Ohrdruf and his wife were forced to visit the place. They disclaimed any definite knowledge of what had happened there, and committed suicide that night.

Protected by smoke fog, Bob Shumway's squad lies
flat on the ground awaiting the order to board the
assault boats for the Rhine' crossing into Germany

Bob Shumway's platoon, in assault boats, crossing the Rhine

Ohrduf, 10 April 1945

TESTIMONY OF VETERAN
A.P. "AL" STEVENS

I had quit high school in my senior year at age 16. In those days, in Massachusetts at least, if a male student left high school after completion of the first half of his senior year in high school with the intent of going to college to get as much college study in before entering the service, the high school was required to award a diploma to the student upon successful completion of his first semester of college.

Taking advantage of this opportunity, I matriculated at Clark University in April of 1943 and went "round the clock" until called to active duty in January 1945 in the U. S. Army Air Corps, having enlisted some months earlier in the cadet program.

During the then prescribed basic infantry training we were given classification tests to determine whether we would receive training as pilots, bombardiers, navigators or gunners. I was fortunate enough to be classified in my choice, navigation.

At this point a minor glitch in events occurred when I became a resident of the base hospital in Biloxi, Mississippi with what was termed "something akin to rheumatic fever", deferring my completion of basic training by some 5 weeks. When I resumed training (on the day my original squadron was shipping out) I found myself in with a group of "rebels" rather than with the New Englanders with whom I had been quartered. This led to interesting times and discussions, particularly with regard to the race issue.

After basic was completed we were told that there had been bad weather in Texas (where the flight schools we were to attend were located) and so there was a backup which would mean that we would have "advanced basic". This became "advanced advanced basic" until we were dispersed - but not to flight school. I personally was sent to Smyrna AFB in Tennessee to work in the public relations office where my sole duty was to read the two newspapers which came to the office, cut out any articles which referred to Smyrna AFB and paste them in a scrapbook. The duty was so onerous that I sought R and R every night in Nashville. Our CO was a Major Davis who was called Mother Davis since he looked after all of our needs - we had a squadron garden which meant the freshest of vegetables, and he saw that we had our eggs cooked to order for breakfast and a choice of two or three beverages at every meal. The whole experience was a most difficult and harrowing one.

This all came to an end when I was sent to Chanute Field in Rantoul, Illinois to attend tech school. My assignment was to the sheet metal area and I was trained to become a "tin knocker", repairing holes in B-17s, B-24s and the new B-29s.

At this point we were told that since the Army had not carried out its end of the bargain, we might either be discharged or go to flight school, get our commissions, and sign on for two more years.

The decision was not a difficult one to make, since I wanted to finish my college program. Thus, on November 1, 1945 I became a free man, having released a WAC for active duty during the term of my enlistment.

ALLEN L. TORREY

FLIGHT TIME
1943-1947
JULY, 2000

I'm putting in writing these memories of my participation in the military during World War II while my recall of that period is still very clear. Those few years played such an important part in the lives of your mother's and my generation that I would like to leave some record of my own military "career" for our family records.

In the fall of 1941 I entered the University of Maine at Orono intending to major in civil engineering. Sylvia began her studies at the University of New Hampshire at the very same time. We had attended Weymouth High School together, although I took my last two years at Fryeburg Academy in Fryeburg, Maine. There I could be under the watchful eye of my brother Ron who was a teacher and coach at the Academy. Sylvia and I had dated on and off for several years. The world events that unfolded drew us much closer together.

In those years at least two years of R.O.T.C. military training was required of all males at any state university. Strangely though, I was never in the program because I did not pass the physical exam. This was odd because I was a first stringer at left guard on the freshman football team. I failed the physical because of "flat feet." This deficiency never arose during all the many physicals I took during flight training.

We always remember where we were on certain memorable dates. For us this was the attack on Pearl Harbor, December 7, 1941. My closest friend was Bob Crabtree who had been my roommate at Fryeburg and started at UMaine with me. Bob's parents lived in the little town of Hancock, Maine, about sixty miles from the University. We often spent weekends there traveling back and forth by hitch-hiking. That Sunday afternoon, on our way back to the university, we first heard the news on the car radio. This news hit us particularly hard, because Bob's oldest brother was then stationed in the Philippines. The Crabtree family lost three of their four sons in the course of the war. Bob was a B-24 pilot who was lost flying out of Italy in early 1945.

With outbreak of the war, college life changed dramatically. Courses were speeded up, there was much more emphasis on physical and military training and classmates began to leave for the services. All young men registered for the draft, but as a college student and only 19 years old, I was temporarily deferred. I was fortunate to line up a good job for the summer of 1942 with some help from my father. That spring of 1942 the navy decided to build a whole new shipyard in Hingham, Mass., as a spin-off from the big Fore River Yard in Quincy where my father had worked for years as a supervisor of engine room drafting. Because of my one year of engineering and the two previous summers of work for the local surveyor, "Uncle" Bert Libby, I got hired as an experienced (?) transit man with the engineering crews laying out the new shipyard. This was a great learning experience for me, the pay was good, lots of overtime and only two miles from home. The engineers I worked with were responsible for all the underground services, water, sewer, gas, electricity, etc.: good training for a future town manager.

The threat of the draft hung over me, especially since I was not in the R.O.T.C. program. I had always been interested in flying. I built many model airplanes and used to hang out at the little airport which later became the site of the new shipyard. One day while I was working at the shipyard a pair of P-40s roared over the yard at a very low altitude. This was probably a staged show for morale purposes, and it did hook me. My father's advice was to wait "until you're drafted." If I had waited, I surely would have ended up in the infantry, flat feet or not. Instead, against my father's wishes, I went to Boston and took the exams for the Aviation Cadet program. I was accepted and told to go home and wait for the call, which would probably come in December. I saw no point in going back to college. I had a good job and it would only be three months until I was called. My father disagreed, and since he was paying the bills, I went back to Maine for the fall semester. By now college was even more hectic with friends leaving daily for the Army or Navy.

I stayed for the full fall semester, and it wasn't a complete waste of time. I passed most of the courses. In fact, I did well in the engineering courses, but flunked calculus. There were many farewell parties and promises to keep in touch. My orders to report finally came. I was to report to the Back Bay Station in Boston early on February 8, 1943. My parents drove me into the station. We, along with a couple hundred other would-be cadets and their respective parents, said our goodbyes and I boarded the train, destination unknown. I expect my mother's last words were to stand up straight and to look to the good side of everything; my father probably urged me to be careful and cautious. I had expected to see some of my college friends who were reporting the same day, but they left from Bangor and our paths did not cross again.

From Boston via troop train I, along with probably two hundred other would-be cadets, debarked in Atlantic City. But we were not "cadets," we were privates in the U.S. Army. The cadet designation would have to wait several more months. It was on this train that I first met Joe Tolland, and because the Army always did things alphabetically, Tolland and Torrey stayed together throughout training and overseas, until the time of Joe's accident. Atlantic City had been turned into a huge basic training base. All the big hotels were taken over and converted to troop housing. Because of the submarine activity off the coast, Atlantic City was in a complete blackout. My memory was that it was cold, wet and very dark. Here we were uniformed, inoculated and drilled. We were marched out to the rifle ranges about five miles away and given instruction using various weapons and introduced to gas masks.

Basic training was supposed to last several months, but suddenly after just three weeks we were back on a train, destination unknown. In one of the many oddities of military life, we got off the train at Northampton, Massachusetts. From the station we were bused to Amherst and to the campus of Mass. State College. There we became the first cohort of the 58th College Training Detachment. We were housed in Lewis and Thatcher Halls, new dorms at the time but still in use today. The purpose of a C.T.D. was twofold, first to bring everyone up to an educational level required for flight training and, second to keep these physically fit and educated young men out of the infantry until there was space in the flight training pipeline.

We didn't get much time off as I recall; I do have memories of going downtown in Amherst a few times. One weekend in late March my mother and father drove over to Amherst from Weymouth, which must have taken all of dad's gas coupons. They brought Sylvia with them and we had lunch at the Lord Jeff. Remember the snapshot of the two of us standing in the yard of the Jeff?

While at Mass. State, the Air Corps decided to begin flight training using civilian instructors and planes. Again luck was with me and I was in the first group to receive flight instruction. This involved a daily trip by school bus over to Barnes Airport in Westfield. We were assigned a civilian instructor. Over the course of a couple of weeks I logged several hours in a Piper Cub, not enough to solo. Every time I drive by Barnes I think of my first flights right here in the Valley. Many of

Sylvia and I in front of the
Lord Jeff. March, 1943

the would-be cadets spent a year or more in the C.T.D.s but here again I was fortunate and found myself in the first group to leave the C.T.D. and move ahead into the Cadet program.

After about six weeks in Amherst a small group shipped out, again by train, to Nashville, Tennessee "classification center" where we at last we were given the choice of pilot, navigator, or bombadier training. Most everybody elected pilot as the other two programs would be available if we did not become pilots. We must have been in Nashville several weeks, but I have no memory of the place at all. I do remember very well the next step in the pipeline called "Preflight." It took place at the dreaded Maxwell Field in Montgomery, Alabama. You can imagine what it was like in July and August. Preflight consisted of a very strenuous physical training program, long cross-country and obstacle courses, a lot of academics, navigation and military, and for me, the hardest of all, "code." I knew the Morse code from back in the Boy Scouts but I could never get the rhythm right so as to pass the thirty word per minute requirement. I must have somehow, as I continued in the program. Every Friday afternoon the entire cadet corps paraded and passed in review, it was quite a sight.

We often got weekend passes and could go into Montgomery overnight. I remember that we could stay at the Salvation Army for a buck, one of the reasons I have always been supportive of them. As a Cadet, the goal of the silver wings and the gold bars was always there. The next step was the first flying school known as "primary."

"Preflight" lasted only two months but I remember well the heat, the drilling and the discipline. The move to primary flying school in Albany, Georgia was like going from day to night. While Albany had a large military presence, the primary school was actually run by civilians under a contract with the Air Corps. It had much, much less "chickenshit," good food, a swimming pool, and a generally more relaxed atmosphere with weekends off. As I look back, I think calculated policy so that we could concentrate on the flight instruction. The instructors were civilians and we flew the Stearman PT-19 biplane; there are still some flying today. The first level was to "solo" after about 8-10 hours of instruction. If you didn't make this step it was off to navigator or bombardier school. My first attempt to solo was a failure; I "ground looped" the Stearman damaging a wing.

A Pt-19. My first solo.

The rest of that day and night I was pretty down expecting to be washed out the next day. It didn't happen, my instructor must have like me or at least he saw some potential, because he gave me a second chance. On the next try I soloed successfully and never looked back. After soloing the emphasis was on acrobatics and short cross-country flights.

One event that happened at Albany was the wedding of my friend Joe Tolland and his long-time girlfriend from Boston. I was the best man. It must have been a success because they had six kids, and we went to their fiftieth anniversary in 1993.

At the end of two months it was off again on the Central Georgia Railroad in cars which had once been used to transport the Confederate forces to war. This time the move was to basic flight training in Greenwood, MS. The training plane at Basic was a BT-12, a low wing monoplane, must faster, with some instruments and a radio. I found it a much more stable aircraft and much easier to land. But we were now back in the army with army instructors. Here we got our first taste of night and instrument flying. We made some cross-country flights, actually landing at a different airfield. After the usual two-month program, it was off again to "Advanced."

Future pilots with the BT-12,
L to R, Timberlake, Tolland, Warren, Torrey

However, before moving on there was another choice to be made; "single engine or multi-engine?" was the question. Joe and I chose multi-engine while the majority opted for single engine, dreaming of becoming hot fighter pilots. My own desire was the B-25, a twin-engine medium bomber the plane made famous by the Doolittle raid on Tokyo. It turned out there were never any B-25 groups in Europe, although they were used in North Africa and in the Pacific.

Our final move in the program was to advanced twin-engine training in Columbus, Mississippi. Both Greenwood and Columbus were in the deep South, buses and toilets were segregated. On weekends we usually went into town. I remember in Columbus buying some whiskey from the local bootlegger and eating large black-market steaks. There were always movies and U.S.O.s for entertainment. Cadets were sort of in-between as we were neither officers nor "G.I.s." Living space off the bases was pretty horrible, but Joe's wife Gert always seemed to find a place and she stayed with us right through to graduation.

The planes we flew at "Advanced" were AT-10's, a small twin-engine made by Beechcraft. One of the big tests at "Advanced" was called single engine operation. The instructor would suddenly reach over and kill one engine to test our procedure skills. There were also a lot of instrument and night cross-countries. But every day we were getting closer to the big day when we would graduate. The reality really set in when we went to the base tailors to be fitted for our new uniforms. We each received an allowance of $300.00 to spend on uniforms and that was just about what they cost.

The big day finally came, February 9, 1944, just one year from the day I left Boston. On that day we received our wings, our gold Second Lieutenant bars, and our future assignments. As I look back on that year, for me to have made it all the way was quite an accomplishment. I came from a pretty sheltered background and was only twenty at graduation.

Our orders, Joe's and mine, were to report to Seymour Johnson Field in Goldsboro, North Carolina, with a 14 days "delay on route." The normal procedure for newly graduated pilots was to report to what was called O.T.U. (Operational Training Units) to learn to fly combat aircraft like B-17s, B-26s, etc. But we had orders to report directly to an overseas training deport. This didn't seem right, we had better enjoy our leaves, so off we went for Boston. By bus, train and plane, the four of us (Gert being several months pregnant) went. My parents met us in Boston. Mother sent me up to town hall to the ration board to get my special allowance of meat, sugar and gas coupons allowed to military on leave. I made good use of the gasoline in my father's car and my mother made good use of the extra rations. I'm sure Sylvia came down from Durham and this led to our becoming engaged.

Sylvia and I.
February, 1944

A word about Sylvia. She of course stayed on at UNH in a very accelerated program that included summer school. This allowed her to graduate in June 1944 instead of 1945. My mother produced a diamond from among the Torrey family treasures which we had made into a ring that Sylvia wears today. Women were expected to perform some kind of war work or service, especially bright college graduates. She could have gone into one of the Women's Armed Services, but she chose to go to Washington where she had an exciting year and more working in Japanese cryptography for the Army Intelligence.

When leave was up it was down to North Carolina for overseas training, whatever that meant. What possible use would we be without the training in operational (combat) aircraft? Overseas training consisted of hikes, overnight camping in tents and generally killing time for about a month. Then it was off to a P.O.E. (point of embarkation) at Fort Hamilton in Brooklyn, New York. There were about thirty of us junior birdmen in the group. We spent two or three weeks at Fort Hamilton doing nothing except going into New York City every evening on the Subway; a nickel each way. There were constant rumors that we would be shipping out the next day. Mother and Sylvia came down from Weymouth on the train to show me the new engagement ring. It was just a day later that things began to move.

From a pier in New York City, we boarded the big Cunard liner *Aquitannia* for our trip across the Atlantic. Because the ship was considered fast, we sailed unescorted. The trip took about six days. Troopships certainly were not the luxury liners they once had been, but as officers we were far more comfortable than the hundreds of troops crammed below. We had two meals per day and spent a lot of time on deck, which meant we must have taken a southerly course, yet when we landed we were in Scotland. Our small group of about thirty new second lieutenants (all pilots) hung together. I think we were the only. Air Corps personnel on board. We wore our leather A-2 jackets all the time to distinguish (show off) our difference. From Grennock, Scotland, we went by train to Stoke-on-Trent, a replacement center where my future would be decided. Without any further training since graduating the most likely assignment would be as co-pilots of a medium bomber, or so we thought. To our surprise we ended up at Grove Army Air Base and the only planes in sight were C-47s. Perhaps some members of the group were disappointed in not being sent to a combat unit but others, myself included, decided it was not a bad situation. The base was near the little village of Wantage, about 20 miles west of Oxford. The outfit was the 326th Ferrying Squadron of the 315th Air Transport Group, a part of the 9th Air Force Service Command.

When we arrived the squadron consisted of about 20 pilots, some "ground pounders," (our name for non-flying officers like weather men) and a flight surgeon, plus the usual complement of mechanics, radio techs, cooks and truck drivers. The pilots were mostly older, a mixed bag of service pilots, experienced pilots who had never gone to army flight school, and a number of Americans who had joined the R.C.A.F and then transferred back to the USAAF. The C.O. and the other pilots must have been surprised to receive a cadre of 30 newly graduated pilots without any advanced training.

The commanding officer of the squadron was a Major Hansen who was a prewar army pilot. He must have screwed up somewhere to only be a major in command of such a group. We were welcomed rather lukewarmly at first, too many new and inexperienced pilots, and too few aircraft. According to my form 5 (pilot's log) I took my first flight since graduation on April 21, 1944, a layoff of two and one-half months. On April 22 I logged nine hours (!) of co-pilot time with four landings. Maybe it was one of our frequent trips to Northern Ireland. My first time logged as a pilot was on May 28th. Obviously we moved ahead very quickly. Our transition from unqualified co-pilots to full pilots was very quick. Late in May we doubled the number of aircraft and by late June we occasionally flew without even a co-pilot. The crew chiefs loved that. If you look at my time sheets you will note much of my logged time was in a C-53-D. This was one of the original DC-3s made for the airlines and did not have the big cargo doors that the military version had. I liked the C-53 because it only had a door big enough for passengers who could get on and off by themselves. On a C-47 the pilot and crew often had to act as baggage handlers.

Loading disposable wing tanks for fighter plane into a C-42.

Also we believed that the C-53 was about ten M.P.H. faster.

A word about the mission of the 315th Air Transport Group: we were a division of the 9th Air Force. The 9th was a tactical air force consisting of fighter squadrons, light and medium bombers, and troop carriers. My squadron's main mission was to support the fighter groups consisting of P-47s and P-51s. Because of their shorter range these groups frequently moved forward as the front lines moved. Our job was to keep them supplied with pilots, engines, bombs, and other high priority supplies. Some in the squadron were called "ferry pilots." Their job was to pick up new planes at the assembly depots and ferry them to the fighter bases. One of our C-47s was assigned every day to be the "taxi shop" whose job it was to retrieve the ferry pilots and return them to our base for another ferrying mission. This was not easy as the ferry pilots were frustrated fighter pilots. They tried to hide with their fighter pilot friends and sneak in on a combat mission.

We were scheduled to fly six days a week with one day off. We usually spent that day in Oxford, which could be reached by public bus from Wantage. Occasionally we went into London by train, staying overnight at the Red Cross Clubs.

The months of April, May and June were exciting times to be in southern England. Every field and country lane was crammed with trucks, tanks and ammunition storage dumps. We knew it wouldn't be long until the invasion. Near the end of May, Joe and I received a very interesting assignment. The two of us, along with a crew chief, a mechanic and a C-47, were placed on detached service and assigned to the "Circus" based at an old RAF base at Thorny Island on the extreme south coast. The "Circus" was a collection of all the aircraft expected to be used by the allies in the invasion. The idea was to parade over the anti-aircraft batteries at various altitudes to acquaint the gunners with the shapes and sizes of our planes. We flew all along the south coast at various altitudes. Fortunately, none of the gunners tried to use us for target practice. It was very different living at an RAF base. The food wasn't very good, but the social life and the living conditions were much better. On the afternoon of June 5th our route took us over Portsmouth harbor. The waters were covered with ships and landing crafts and for the first time we saw they were full of troops. Joe remarked that it looked like the invasion would begin soon, the understatement of the war. Next morning we were awakened to the news that the big event had begun. There we were, about as close to the invasion beaches as we could get and we were "grounded." After three days the "Circus" was disbanded and we were ordered back to Grove. We never knew how we happened to draw this assignment, but it was an interesting experience. As soon as Omaha Beachhead was secured, a temporary airstrip called "T-1" was prepared just above the invasion beach. High priority cargo and personnel flights to the Beach began within a couple of days. At first the return flight

Our squadron with-Red Cross ambulances. Chartes, France.

cargos were medical evacuees. We all wanted to cross the channel but for the first week or more the senior officers of the squadron took all the flights.

My first trip across was about June 18th. Looking down on the invasion beaches was a sight always to remember. To land on the strip we had to enter into an alley formed by barrage balloons with our own anti-aircrafts tracking us onto the strip until we landed on the strip. If the Germans had only realized how vulnerable we were they could have caused havoc. Fortunately they never took advantage of the situation, presumably saving their Luftwaffe for things to come.

Within a couple more weeks our engineers had constructed a more permanent airfield designed to be an air freight terminal and named it "A-1". When Sylvia and I visited the Normandy beaches in 1998, I tried to locate the site of these first two strips but couldn't find any trace or reference to them. I concluded that the first strip, "T-1", was now a part of the beautiful and moving American Military Cemetery at Omaha Beach.

During the summer and fall we continued to operate out of the base at Grove. We often spent nights "on the road," that is, our missions were often listed as R.O.N. meaning "remain over night." The goal was to not fly an empty aircraft if possible, just like a trucking company today. For example, we would leave Grove with a cargo for some Ninth Air Force base somewhere in southern England, pick up another cargo for transport to an advanced fighter base in France, pick up a couple of P-47 engines and take them up to Burtonwood near Manchester for reconditioning. We would stay overnight at the base and pick up a cargo the next day. These trips could stretch out for several days before we got back to the home base.

Just as everybody wanted a trip to the Beach in June, now the goal was to get to Paris, which was liberated in mid-August. Shortly, Paris trips became routine. There were four airfields around the city that we used regularly. I took a picture of four C-47s lined up at LeBouget, the field where Lindbergh landed in 1927. The photo illustrates how extensively the Allies made use of the C-47.

Four c-47s up at LeBourget, France. L to R, USSR,
USA (my X748), RAF and French Air Force.

In the late fall my pal Joe Tolland transferred over to the ferrying section of the group because he was tired of driving C-47s. He was ferrying a B-26 to a light bomber base in Belgium when his plane caught fire on the ground. They all escaped, but Joe was badly burned about the face and hands. Because I was his closest friend and knew his wife so well I was given permission to visit Joe in the field hospital. I took an L4 (a Piper Cub used for artillery spotting) up to a base in Belgium and located Joe's hospital. He looked pretty bad when I first saw him, bandaged from the waist up. As soon as he was well enough to travel he was flown back to the special hospital at Valley Forge where over the next couple of years he had a lot of skin grafts and plastic surgery.

We also frequented Villacoublay on the south side of Paris and later Orly, which became the first transatlantic base for Paris. In early fall it was decided our operations should be based in France and we relocated to Creil, an old Luftwaffe base some twenty-five miles northeast of Paris. There were no permanent buildings except a large old chateau that was taken over for group headquarters with the officer's club in the cellar. We were housed in what were called winterized tents, that is they had wooden floors and sidewalls covered by an army tent. We were four to a tent with a coal stove in the middle. Joe, Duke Parker, Bob Wilson and I were tent mates. By scavenging and stealing we made our tent as comfortable as possible.

We settled in at Creil and it remained our main base until the war ended and we moved into Germany. We lived pretty well. Champagne was quite available as were cigarettes and one bottle of scotch per month. Since I didn't smoke I regularly traded my cigarette ration for scotch. On our day off we could often pick up a flight or truck ride into Paris.

Myself in front of Cleopatra's Needle, Paris. Summer, 1944.

Many of our missions involved trips back to England. I remember Christmas of 1944. We had a flight to Burtonwood on the 24th according to my Form 5. My crew and I went into Manchester and holed up at the Red Cross clubs.

The next morning (Christmas Day) there was no chance of flying because of the fog and low clouds. In fact we were so "weathered in" we didn't get off the ground until the 30th. This was when the Battle of the Bulge was at its height. Much of the Germans' early success was because all of our aircraft on both the continent and in England were grounded. It was so foggy in Manchester that I recall seeing a man on foot with a lantern preceding the buses. My contribution to the Battle of the Bulge was nil.

In early January as the Bulge was winding down I drew a mission to Luxembourg to pick up a number of captured German Luftwaffe pilots and take them to England for interrogation. The runway there was snow covered (no snow plows). We loaded up our passengers and the one M.P. sent along to guard them. My crew and I were unarmed although we officers were supposed to be wearing a .45. I told the crew chief to load up the flare pistol, and if there was any trouble shoot it into the passenger cabin. Actually, I think the P.O.W.s were quite happy to be going to England and out of the war for good.

In February, 1945, one year from the date of our initial commissioning, most of my original group were promoted to 1st Lieutenant. This meant silver bars and a small raise for us.

Creil, France. Winter 1944-1945: Front L to R: Johnson, Wilson, Davis, Tolland, Hutchinson Standing L to R: Martin, Dragon, Fields, Lewis, Rogers, Slawson, Dunham, Porter, Silva, Ward

As spring came on we flew further and further into Germany, finally crossing the Rhine. Our bases were generally former Luftwaffe installations hastily repaired by our engineers. Our home was still at Creil when V-E day occurred. I happened to have the day off and we headed into Paris for the celebration. Sometime during the evening I got very sick to my stomach and sought help in one of the Red Cross clubs. Eventually an army ambulance came for me and took me to the American Hospital of Paris. How they got the ambulance through the crowds I don't recall. I was examined and scheduled for an appendectomy the next morning, but when morning came I was quite recovered. I kept my appendix but they did keep me there for three days for observation and rest. This was the only time I was ever hospitalized until recent years.

In early summer (1945) our group made its final move into the former Luftwaffe base at Ansbach, Germany, near Nurenburg. The base had been a German training base and had never been bombed or shot up much during the war. It had very substantial and comfortable buildings, especially the officers' club and quarters. It was quite an improvement after living for a year or more in either Quonset huts or winterized tents. We celebrated V-J day in the officers' mess with a really big party.

Now that the war in Europe was finished there was a rapid redeployment of many of the fighter and bomber groups. Some went directly home to be reequipped and sent to the Pacific. But the war against Japan continued only a few more months. Our transport group still had plenty of work, but we became more of an airline. We began to fly regular routes on schedule and transporting troops on R & R (rest and relaxation). One of the most popular of the R & R trips was to the French Riviera. We could make it down to the Riviera and back in one day but we tried hard to avoid one day round trips in hopes of staying overnight in Cannes or Nice. We used excuses like bad weather over the mountains, or no landing lights at our home base. The airstrip at Nice was really on the Beach, the closest we ever came to a water landing. To increase our passenger capacity the group received several stripped down B-17s hastily converted into transports. We had a former B-17 instructor pilot in the squadron, Captain Bill Field, and he checked out several of us in our first four-engine aircrafts. My Form 5 indicates that I began to log some instruction and co-pilot time in the B-i7 beginning in June of 1945.

We also qualified for R & R's ourselves, once for a week in Cannes, another to Lake Annacy in the French Alps, and one week in Switzerland. The latter came about because of my only serious accident. I drew a mission to Frankfort to transport a load of high-point NCOs to France to start them on their way home. I was also check-riding a new pilot, which meant that I was in command but in the co-pilot seat. As we started down the runway at Frankfurt-am-Main, but had not reached flying speed, we blew the right-hand tire. We chopped the power and the plane veered to the right, narrowly missing a work crew digging trenches for runway lighting. We finally came to a stop. We had a pretty scared bunch of passengers but no injuries. That plane never flew again. When I got back to Ansbach I had to be cleared by the flight surgeon before flying again. He recommended I take some time off and there just happened to be a couple of slots for a one week R & R to Switzerland, I lucked out. It seemed like heaven after war torn France and Germany. I remember well the pastries and chocolate, also a couple of days in the ski resort at Davos. Unfortunately it was September and too early for snow.

Later in the fall, while waiting for shipping orders, four of us along with a sergeant as driver requisitioned an Army command car and toured southern Germany and into Austria. We spent a day and night in Garmisch, rode a cable car to the top of the Zugspitz, toured the Auschwitz concentration camp and visited Berchesgarten, site of Hitler's mountain retreat. His chalet, called the Eagle's Nest was pretty well destroyed by then, but we lined up in what had been his living room and we pissed on the floor, a very brave act on our parts.

By late October we were eagerly awaiting our shipping orders. I flew 25 hours in the month of October; my last flight in a C-47 was October 19th. I did fly five more hours in an L-4, just to pass the time. My total flying time in Europe came to 1,495:20 hours. This was quite an accumulation of flying hours compared to the time bomber or fighter pilots would have totaled.

In late November our orders came and we traveled by plane and truck to the French port of Le Harve, the main point of embarkation. We were at camp "Philip Morris." The camps were all named for cigarettes! We spent several weeks in inactivity and boredom. Finally our ship came in and we boarded the S.S. *Vassar Victory* for the homeward trip. These quarters were pretty basic, although we had it better than most of the troops aboard. Since we were on our way home morale was high and the fear of submarines was over. Our ship sailed into Boston Harbor and docked at the army base. As we entered the harbor I could actually make out the profile of Weymouth Great Hill where I grew up. We went by train to Camp Myles Standish in Taunton for a day. When we went through the

15 Lovell Street.

serving line for our first meal in this country we were surprised to find that German P.O.W.s were serving the food.

The next day I shipped out to Fort Devens for final discharge. I called home from there and the next day my mother, father and Sylvia came out to pick me up. It was a Saturday, about December 21st, that I finally arrived at 15 Lovell Street after an absence of almost three years. I was actually on what was called "terminal leave" and on the army payroll until mid-February.

There was no question but that I would immediately return to college and if I hurried I could resume at the beginning of the spring semester. As a returning veteran I was guaranteed a place at UMaine. I don't recall that I ever considered a transfer to another University. But first there were big decisions that had to be made. Number one was the fact that Sylvia and I had now been engaged for two years. Her job in Washington had ended about the same time I got home. She either had to look for a new job, probably teaching, or she could marry me and share the unknown future. She chose the latter.

Financially, I could go back to college because of the "G.I. Bill" which would cover the cost of tuition and books, plus a small living allowance ($90 per month for married veterans). I had saved some money from my army pay and Sylvia also had saved, plus she had an ample wardrobe from her Washington days. I didn't. In fact, I had a hard time getting outfitted, hence the decision to be married in uniform. We made the big decision about Christmas and set the wedding date for January 19th, a tight schedule for parents. Now all we had to do was for me to get enrolled at UMaine with all the necessary paperwork and find an affordable place to live in Orono, Maine. The wedding went off fine, although the church was very cold. My parents loaned us their car so we could have a brief honeymoon in North Conway, including a day or two of skiing at Cranmore. Then we drove to Orono where we were promised a used trailer in a new "G.I." village hastily being erected near the campus. It was cheap ($19.00 per month) and within walking distance of my classes and downtown Orono. We signed up for the trailer and returned to Weymouth to get ready for the big move. We must have taken the train from Boston to Bangor and a bus to Orono.

In any event we were there in time to start classes for the spring semester along with hundreds of others who were resuming or starting college for the first time. The trailer colony was filled with young marrieds. For the men who had lived under similar conditions it was ok, but it must have been very hard for the wives. We did not have running water or a toilet in the trailer. We had to go to the central building for those items and for a shower. The young couple in the next trailer seemed friendly; their names were Harrington (Ben and Donna) from Amherst, Massachusetts. Our paths were to cross again. The Harringtons later moved back to Amherst and we continued our close friendship through all these years.

A couple of items I should mention. Prior to my military service I was planning to major in civil engineering. My summer jobs also were in that direction. However, when I reenrolled at UMaine, I considered a change to Liberal Arts, aiming for a career in government like the state department. I went for an interview with the head of the government department (Edward F. Dow). He looked over my record and suggested Public Management, a new major aimed at municipal government administration. He pointed out that my year and a half of civil engineering would be valuable in the town/city management field. Ed Dow was not only a very good professor but he became a mentor for quite a number of town and city managers throughout New England and beyond.

I should also report that I did some more flying after my discharge. While at the University I joined the 132nd Fighter Squadron of the Maine Air National Guard stationed at Dow Field on the outskirts of Bangor. The squadron was equipped with P-47N Thunderbolts. The outfit also had a "utility flight" consisting of one C-47 and several AT-6s and L-5s. To get flight pay we had to fly four hours per month and go to two weeks of summer camp. The pay was good, especially since with a wife and two little boys, Allen and Philip, we could always use more money. By now we were living in a two-bedroom apartment on campus with running water, a bathroom and a coal stove.

My Form 5 shows I flew the C-47 a few times each month beginning in October 1947 and continuing through to May of 1948. I logged more time in the AT-6, but the best way to get in my flying time was to take up an L-5 and fly around Maine an hour or more on a nice day. My most harrowing event took place during the summer camp, when some lamebrain decided I should check out in a P-47. I had never flown a single engine fighter and the P-47N was the largest and heaviest propeller driven fighter the U.S.A.F. ever had. After about a half hour of cockpit instruction on the ground I took off, circled around Bangor a couple of times, and got the beast back on the ground safely. My form shows I logged 30 minutes that day. When we moved to Lancaster, New Hampshire in May of 1948 I had to resign my commission in the Maine Air Guard, a good thing because when the Korean War started the 132nd was the first Air Guard outfit to be called back to active duty.

In retrospect I was very fortunate in my military career. I was never in combat. I don't think I was ever fired at and I never had a serious accident. We did accumulate a lot of flight time and we did fly many hours in the "combat zones." I have included a page from my Form 5 for the month of September 1944 which was typical of our activities. It shows the dates, types of aircraft flown, number of landings and accumulated flight time. We were rewarded with the Air Medal and several battle stars to wear on our theater ribbon. The stars later proved valuable when adding up points for discharge.

As I look back on the whole experience the biggest hazard we faced was weather. We always had to get a briefing from our meteorological officers and they were very good and also cautious. But without today's radar and little information from the east, we took some awful chances. Most of our navigation was by "contact," that is following along on a line drawn on the map observing checkpoints like cities, or where we left the English coast, or where we crossed the Rhine. We also had a radio compass which allowed us to get a compass bearing on some airfields. We tried to avoid instrument and night flying, as there were no control or fixed flight rules as there are today. We also had some tricks. I remember that you could get into Grove in bad weather by closely following the railroad tracks to a certain point which led into the main runway. We took a lot of chances and were sent out on missions when we shouldn't have been sent. There was also very little direct supervision or rigid military discipline. All in all, the assignment to the 315th Air Transport Group turned out well.

Considering my age and life experience up to the time I entered the service, I'm sure those three years did a great deal for my personal growth and development. When I think back on those years and the responsibilities and dangers which I was exposed to ages 19-22 I was also very lucky. I saw much of our own country and much of Europe. I met many young men from many different backgrounds, I also crossed the Atlantic both ways by ship - kind of odd that we didn't fly. As I described earlier, our little group was sent overseas without any training beyond flight school. The assignment to the Air Transport Group turned out for the best. Without any combat aircraft training, the best we could have expected was as a replacement co-pilot slot in a bomber group. The C-47 was a good, reliable airplane and relatively easy to learn to fly. The missions were varied and generally useful. And we did get in a lot of flight time! I am proud of the fact I made it through the rigorous Aviation Cadet Program and earned my wings and my commission. I also made some important decisions on my own. I stood up against my father when I took the initiative to join the cadet program, and with Sylvia's support we chose to marry young and have a family, although a little quicker than we expected. It also turned out that the career path I chose at UMaine turned out to be fulfilling and successful.

I have written all this for limited circulation to the family, not because of any great pride in what I did in the WWII days, but because earlier generations did not leave much in the way of their personal histories. They left material things, but very little about their own lives, a fact which has always been disappointing.

ATTACHMENT A

A page from my Form 5 for September 1944. By checking dates in Column 1 it appears that I flew 27 out of 30 days that month. Column 2 shows the type of plane; C-47's, CS3's and on September 17th, 20 minutes in a UC-64, a single engine high-wing utility plan we all disliked to fly. Column 3 shows the number of landings that day, 8 landings and 6:30 hours of pilot time on September 19th. Total pilot time for the month was 11955 hours.

INDIVIDUAL FLIGHT RECORD

(1) SERIAL NO. O-822855 (2) NAME Torrey Allen L. (3) RANK 2d Lt (4) AGE 92
(5) PERS. CLASS 18 (6) BRANCH Air Corps (7) STATION AAF 519
(8) ORGANIZATION ASSIGNED IX AFSC 1st Trans. Gp. (Prov) 315th Trans. Sq.
(9) ORGANIZATION ATTACHED
(10) PRESENT RATING & DATE Pilot 8 February 1944 (11) ORIGINAL RATING & DATE Pilot 8 Feb 44
(12) TRANSFERRED FROM (13) FLIGHT RESTRICTIONS None
(15) TRANSFERRED TO (14) TRANSFER DATE

(17) MONTH September 4

DAY	AIRCRAFT TYPE, MODEL & SERIES	NO. LANDINGS	COMMAND PILOT	CO-PILOT	FIRST PILOT C/A	FIRST PILOT DAY	FIRST PILOT NIGHT
1	C-47-A	5			12:40	2:40	
3	C-47	6				6:20	
5	C-47	6			2:05	5:05	
6	C-53	6			2:15	3:10	
7	C-47	4			2:25	2:25	
8	C-47	5			2:20	2:20	
10	C-47	6			2:45	2:40	
12	C-47	1			1:50		
13	C-53	7			3:05	3:05	
14	C-53	2				1:10	
11	C-47	2				3:35	
15	C-53	5			2:25	2:30	
16	C-53	2			1:45	1:50	
17	C-47	2			:50	:50	
17	C-53	1				:40	
17	UC-64	1				:20	
18	C-53	6			1:05	1:10	
19	C-53	8				6:30	
20	C-53	2			1:35	1:35	
21	C-53	6			2:40	2:45	
22	C-53	1			:30	:25	
24	C-47	5			2:30	1:50	
25	C-47	2			1:05	1:00	
26	C-47	4			2:30	2:30	:50
27	C-47	3			2:45	2:40	
28	C-47	3			2:45	2:45	
29	C-47	3			2:45	2:45	
23	C-47	4			1:55	2:00	
30	C-47	4			3:00	3:00	

CERTIFIED CORRECT:
WILLIAM B. BARRETT
1st Lt. AC.
Opns O
315th TS

COLUMN TOTALS 49:30 69:35 :50

	(42) TOTAL STUDENT PILOT TIME	(43) TOTAL FIRST PILOT TIME	(44) TOTAL PILOT TIME
(37) THIS MONTH		69:35 :50	119:05 :50
(38) PREVIOUS MONTHS THIS F. Y.		146:05 1:00	171:40 1:00
(39) THIS FISCAL YEAR		215:40 1:50	290:45 1:50
(40) PREVIOUS FISCAL YEARS	252:50	67:50 :25	433:35 1:00
(41) TO DATE	252:50	283:30 2:15	724:20 2:50

ATTACHMENT B

News item from the Amherst Record, March 3, 1943 describing the arrival of the first group of would-be cadets at Massachusetts State College (now UMass). The article does not give the size of the first group, but I think we numbered about 250.

THE AMHERST RECORD, WEDNESDAY, MARCH 3, 1943

First Group of Army Air Corps Cadets Arrive at State College

The first group of Army Air Corps cadets have arrived at State College for a course of study and more will arrive later. The cadets are housed in Thatcher and Lewis dormitories. More than 80 members of the State College faculty will assist in teaching.

Dr. Ralph A. Van Meter, whom President Hugh P. Baker of the college recently appointed associate dean in charge of the army teaching program, stated that instructors have volunteered from many college departments and have already begun special study to fit themselves for the particular requirements of the army education program. Refresher courses have been offered in several subjects to train instructors for the program.

The curriculum for the Army Air Forces college training program includes instruction of soldiers in mathematics, physics, history, geography, English, and Civil Air Regulations. A total of 464 hours of academic instruction will be given each student during the course at the college. Approximately 1000 soldiers are expected to be in attendance when the program reaches full volume within the next few weeks.

Military training will be carried on by the commissioned and non-commissioned personnel assigned to the college to direct the military aspects of the training,

pervise the soldiers outside of the classroom. In charge of this phase of the program is Capt. Dewey W. Couri of the A.A.F.

Members of the college physical education department and faculty members qualified in first aid, will instruct the trainees in medical aid and physical education.

The Army Air Force curriculum as forwarded to the college also provides for a number of elective courses similar to those regularly offered by the college. These will be planned later according to need.

The academic instruction program is divided as follows: mathematics, 80 hours; physics, 180 hours; history, 60 hours; geography, 60 hours; English, 60 hours; and Civil Air Regulations, 24 hours. All courses will emphasize the practical aspects of the subject matter and particularly those which will lead to an increased understanding of the more technical training which will later be given to the air crew members at army flight schools. An additional 140 hours of training will be given each student in physical education and medical aid. Basic military indoctrination will occupy 150 hours under direction of the army personnel stationed at the college.

During the final period of training

ATTACHMENT C

The citation accompanying my Air Medal Award. There were 17 pilots and 8 sergeants receiving the award, August 20, 1945.

IX AIR FORCE SERVICE COMMAND

The Air Medal

is awarded

Allen L. Torrey

First Lieutenant, O-822855, Air Corps

by direction of the President, under the provisions of Army Regulation 600-45 as amended, and pursuant to authority vested in me by the Commanding General, Ninth Air Force.

Citation

First Lieutenant Allen L. Torrey, while serving with the Army of the United States, distinguished himself by meritorious achievement while participating in aerial flights from 1 May 1944 to 31 October 1944. During this period he flew a total of 455 hours in the completion of 70 vital transport missions to landing strips bordering enemy-occupied territory in France and in Germany. In the execution of these duties, he displayed courage and a noteworthy flying skill and through his accomplishments he effected a definite contribution to the successful realization of the mission of his organization. Entered military service from Massachusetts.

MYRON R. WOOD
BRIGADIER GENERAL, U.S.A.
COMMANDING

G. O. No. 93, Dated 20 Aug 1945

CONRAD A. WOGRIN

Enlisted December 14, 1942
Honorable Discharge January 26, 1946

THE SECOND WORLD WAR AS I SAW IT

On December 6th,1941 I was 17 years old and was anticipating graduation from high school in January.. My life was very much in order. On graduation I had a job in the Engineering! Drafting office of the Telephone Company (which paid the magnificent amount of $80 per month). I surely would gain admission to at least one of the Colleges to which I had applied. and with the money I could save by September and perhaps a scholarship my future seemed assured.

On December 7th my view of the future, along with one hundred and fifty million other Americans, was significantly less complacent. We were at war and not doing very well. All evidence inducated a long struggle with out a clear victory in sight. The Selective Service Act of 1940 set the draft age at 21 but that surely would be lowered to 18. Before my birthday in April it was. By then I had indeed received admission to Yale with a very generous scholarship. Yale had gone to an accelerated program so I started my college career in July, 1942 and if allowed to complete to a Bachelors degree would finish in January 1945, a mere two and a half years later

My ambition was to become a mathematician, physicist or electrical engineer. All of the advice from elders was to stay in school as men with such training would be needed. A number of programs, such as the Navy V12, which were designed to keep men in school while they trained to become officers, were announced to start in the summer of 1943. In those days one requirement for command was 20/20 vision. I didn't qualify. The Army offered a program which required enlisting in the US Army Enlisted Reserve Corps. Their announced plan was to leave one in school until one earned a degree or until the unlikely event that there was a critical need for manpower. I chose enlistment rather than count on a deferment issued by a Draft Board. I enlisted on Dec 12, 1942. One month later the Army changed its mind and started calling us to active duty. That was my first lesson in the ways of the Army!

My orders did not come until late May after I had finished my third semester of college. On a regular basis during that spring term we had farewell parties for our departing friends. It was 'difficult to devote ones self to serious study, for at any moment you could be gone. During that semester I took a non-credit course in radio electronics and an intensive physical conditioning course. The first of these was to be of importance later in my army career but the second helped immediately. In June 1943 I was in Louisiana in infantry basic training. I was in superb condition and did not have the hard time that so many of my fellow trainees suffered. I thought I was a good candidate for OCS. That's not what happened. I was transferred to a Railway Operating Battalion that was training in the same camp. I learned how to climb telephone poles and string copper wire. I also learned how to set charges of explosives so as to efficiently blow up railroad cars, engines and track. Our final exam produced a magnificent explosion; there were pieces of railroad flying all over the place. Why when preparing to defeat the enemy we spent so much time learning how to retreat was a pu771e to me. Nevertheless, all of this added up to nothing.

One hot day I was called to the Captain's office. He informed that I was being transferred to the ASTP (Army Specialized Training Program) and would proceed immediately to the Arkansas State College in Jonesboro, Arkansas. Was this to be where I would continue my education in mathematics, or physics or engineering? No This is where I was examined for placement. I was assigned to the introductory course in engineering at the Michigan College of Mines and Technology in Houghton, Michigan. When I questioned the assignment, they agreed that I possibly had completed most of the courses but thought that my age precluded me from more advanced education. It is difficult to counter that sort of logic. So from a steamy hot summer of infantry and ralroading in Louisiana I was assigned to one of the coldest places in the US for the winter, a peninsula protruding into Lake Superior. The nearest place of any size, other than the twin town Hancock across the bay, was Ishpeming. As I recall it only snowed once that winter in Houghton. It started snowing the day we arrived in October and when we left in March, it was still snowing. Overall, it was not a bad time. I did very well in my courses. (All were repeats of material I had completed only a few months earlier at Yale). No one asked about my previous education so the faculty was impressed. I did learn how to get around on snowshoes and the people of the town were most cordial. Every Sunday each one of us received an invitation to dinner. We were surrogates for their own sons who were elsewhere in the service of their country.

I was not surprised or disappointed when the Army again had a change of mind. In March, the program was cancelled. I was assigned to the Signal Corps School in Fort Monmouth, New Jersey. This is where my real Army career started

I applied for the Officer Candidate School but had to first complete the basic radio and electronics courses. This did not take long. With the course I had taken at Yale, I was able to take the final exams for most of the work. Did I get assigned to the OCS? No! The school was full and I was placed on a waiting list, To fill my time I was given a course in the operation and maintenance of a machine which could send Morse Code by striking the keys of a typewriter and could receive Morse Code and produce the typed letters. It was called a Boehme Automatic Morse Machine. There was not a single vacuum tube in the entire machine. I was an expert in a machine that was invented in the First World War Oh well I would soon be in OCS. Hall! Not so! Because of this specialty, I was needed immediately in England.

The way to get to England quickly was to go to Camp Crowder in Missouri, get new equipment including a real helmet and a rifle, get a superficial physical examination and then wait until space was found for transport. When I shipped out I was a private first class carrying my own orders. All I knew was that I was going to England to join the 3118 Signal Service Battalion, whatever that was. When I boarded a troopship at night at a dock in New Jersey, I experienced the loneliest feeling I have ever had. I was not with anyone I knew or with whom I would serve and had no idea what the future held. For the first time in my life I was an anonymous cog in a wheel that I was not even sure was round.

The trip was not bad. We traveled in a convoy of ships which stretched as far as could be seen in every direction. After twelve eventless days, we docked in Cardin, Wales. During the trip we did get some news, the most important being that D-day had occurred. From Cardiff we went to a replacement depot near Coventry. There, for two days I avoided the people who were eagerly grabbing-up warm bodies to fill the gaps left by losses on Utah and Omaha beaches. Since I was carrying my own orders, I stubbornly refused to give them up to any officer not connected to the 3118th Signal Service Battalion. It also helped that my specialty was a Boehme machine. When quizzed I merely replied that I could not answer. Nothing like a little secrecy.That along with the fact that my rifle was a carbine rather than an M-1 seemed to save me from returning to the infantry.

On the third day I was found by a Sergeant from the 3118`, During a rapid Jeep ride to Bushy Park in London I learned that the invasion was successful, that my new unit would soon go to France and that the 3118` operated the communications for the Supreme Headquarters Allied Expeditionary Force (SHAEF). Wow! I was working for Eisenhower. My real military career had started.

At the company to which I was assigned no one had ever heard of a Boehme machine and there was no indication that such equipment was scheduled to be added to the TO. No matter, I was apparently capable of fixing faulty radio receivers and transmitters. The team I was to work with was already in France at a place called

Joulaville but I would not immediately join them. I was given a brief introduction to our mission, to the Signal Center in London and some instruction on how we would be working closely with the British. This was all interesting stuff and I did experience some of the buzz bombs that were flying over and dropping on London.

I did not go to France until late August. From Bushy Park we were transferred to an estate somewhere in Sussex to await transport. There was nothing to do but sit. After an interminable wait, early on a bright morning we boarded a transport ship that appeared to be a converted ferryboat. By late afternoon we were off the coast of France. The shore looked like a big cliff. Suddenly a group of landing craft appeared at the side of the boat. We received instructions on the spot on how to get from our deck to the LC some ten or more feet below. Throw your durne bag into the LC as it bangs against the boat. Climb down the cargo net to a point just above where the two boats collide. Just before a collision jump. We all made it with at most a few sprained ankles.

We could not see anything as we made our way to shore. We arrived with a crunch, the front dropped open and we stepped off into some shallow water. We had landed on Omaha Beach. The visible impact was profound. A war had gone by here two and a half months earlier. The beach was covered with the battlements built by the Germans and with the debris of D-Day .. Looking across the beach at the cliff made me wonder how the invasion had succeeded. It must have been a horrible experience requiring unimaginable courage and commitment to a cause.

It started to rain as we made our way up a road that took us to the top of the cliff. We were able to get our pup tents up before it got dark. We were each carrying enough rations to have some nourishment. That brief encounter with the site of the battle stuck in my mind all night. For the first time I had seen why war is hell. For the next ten months I could not help but think of the misery that the guys up front were experiencing. Whatever would be my job I promised myself that I would do it to the best of my ability.

Much to our surprise we were awakened at first light by a sergeant and truck driver who had been searching for us all night I finally was with my unit.. The team I joined was responsible for the communications with the Headquarters of the Armies, the US First, Third ,Seveth and Ninth and the British Second and Canadian First. The team had been with Eisenhower since Africa. I was the green young kid.

At the end of August we moved to Versailles where SHAEF was set up in the Petit Ecurie of the Palace We were barracked in the Academy at St. Cyre. Not bad. It was only a short train ride into Paris. The picture was from the top  of the Eiffel Tower where we had a transmitter and antenna.

This was a rather cushy place to fight a war. But this only lasted until October when our team went to Rheims to set up communications for SHAEF (forward) in a school house. This was the battle commnd center for SHAEF until the war ended. General Beddel Smith, Eisenhower's chief of staff, the officer who was always in his office, probably felt we would function better without the distractions and comforts of Versailles and Paris. I think he was right.

I helped set up the radio room shown here. Each station was a radio connection to a specific Army General's Headquarters. It was

manned 24 hours a day. It is hard to think that in the early forties the most reliable method of communications was telegraphy using Morse code. Everything was encrypted. What the operator got from the code room was a senseless sequence of letters on a sheet of paper. He mentally translated this to the Morse Code, that he keyed into the transmitter. What they received was a senseless string of letter codes and typed the letters on a sheet of paper, which was sent to the code room. I admired their ability to do this for hours on end. On May 6, 1945 I was in this room when the first message of surrender was received from Admiral Doenitz, Hitler's designated successor. It was shortly after Hitler died. At that moment his death was rumored but not known for fact. The operator who received the message was startled to receive a message in plain English. (The Germans apparently knew about this network, Had they been able to crack the code?) The message was immediately taken upstairs to General Smith. In moments he and other officers of his stafffilled that little radio room. I cleared out. There were other types of communications in SHAEF (forward). Land line teletype systems to Paris and London, radio communications to WAR in Washington and others. We used domestic lines wherever they were operational.

In November of 1944 the Colonel commanding the 3118th gave me an assignment. In order to have better control of the communications and to more efficiently clear troubles he wanted to have a control center which could take over any faulty communication path thus relieving the operating room from interruption of their tasks. He asked if I could figure out how to use available equipment to achieve such a center. I came up with a plan for rewiring standard Army telephone switchboards which I had seen stacked up in the supply dump. He gave me a new title and I went to work. Before the task was completed the war had progressed through the Battle of the Bulge and our armies had begun the invasion of Germany. So again in Early April our team was transferred to Frankfort Germany where we set up the new communication center in the I. G. Farben Geselshaft building. Although we had taken our jury rigged gear with us, in Franfort we found a telephone center which had been destroyed by bombing while underconstruction. It contained crates full of very nice gear. We abandoned what we brought and built the control center from this newly acquired treasure trove.

The first picture shows the center the day it went into operation around May 1st. The second picture shows how it had grown by December 1945 when I left to go home for discharge.

One day in June I had been working all night I got a call from the company clerk that I had to come back to the Barracks. I responded that I was busy and could not make it. The next message was from the Captain saying I must report to his office immediately. Again I refused because I was in the middle of some important work. The next message was from the Colonel telling me that his jeep was on its way and I was to get my ass to

the barracks immediately. Since the Colonel out ranked me I went. Much to my surprise there was a full Battallion Parade and I, with several others, was decorated.

CITATION FOR BRONZE STAR MEDAL

Technician Fifth Grade Conrad A Wogrin (Army Serial No. 11092686, Signal Corps, United States Army), for meritorious service in connection with military operations, as noncommissioned officer in charge of technical layout of installations at Supreme Headquarterters, Allied Expeditionary Force (Forward), 3118[1] Signal Service Group, from 15 November 1944 to 15 March 1945. Technician Fifth Grade Wogrin's deft supervision of technical signal installations and his improvisation in combining available equipment with captured enemy material contributed to the continuing efficiency of vital radio communications. His excellent leadership and perseverance were of great value to operations and were consistent with the best traditions of the service. Entered military service from Connecticut.

According to the dates on the citation I was decorated for work accomplished while in Rheims. I think it was for what I did in Frankfort. At the time of the decoration I was a Technician Fourth Grade. When I left Frankfort in December I had the rank of Technical Sergeant. I left the service feeling that I had served as well as I could. I felt lucky to have been one of the group of six that served every one on the front lines. The ones on the front lines deserve the gratitude of us all.

From the landing on Omaha Beach until leaving Europe some eighteen months later we saw a great deal of rubble. The worst was in Germany. In Frankfurt there was a swath through the center of the city a quarter of a mile wide wide in which all buildings were destroyed. After a while one does not see the total destruction. My last view of Europe was the Harbor of', Havre. It was a cold January morning. We waited as the liberty ship which would transport us home came in to dock with the tide because the locks were not functioning. On a pier opposite there was a great tangle of the steel girders which at one time had been a a large building. High on the pile there was a single man banging with a hammer. It seemed so futile. It struck me then that Germany and other places in Europe were beyond repair. I am thankful for the magnificent effort that has rebuilt those cities. None of that complete destruction is visible now.

France, 1945

Reims, France, 1945

Eisenhower and Truman in Frankfurt, Germany, 1945.
Air Force One had stopped in Frankfurt to pick up
Eisenhower en route Potsdam Conference. In background
is a C-54, the first Air-Force One to be used as such
by a sitting President and Commander in Chief.